D1370262

GO FIND!

Training Your Dog to Track

GO FIND!

Training Your Dog to Track

by

L. Wilson Davis

Tenth Printing—1987

HOWELL BOOK HOUSE INC.
230 Park Avenue
New York, N.Y. 10169

To my Wife

ANNE

without whose constant attention to the coffee pot and telephone on Tuesday mornings, this book would never have been finished.

Contents

About the Author   9

Introduction   17

Fundamentals of Training   21

       Lines of Communication . . . Common Sense in Training . . . Timing . . . Consistency . . . Correction and Praise . . . The Key to Success

Basic Control Exercises   31

       The Need for Obedience . . . Heel . . . Stay . . . Down . . . Recall . . . Come . . . Retrieving . . . Correction . . . Repetition . . . Training Devices

The Natural Basis of Tracking   59

       The Dog Knows How to Scent . . . Ground and Airborne Trails . . . Sebum . . . Diversionary Tests . . . Weather and Terrain . . . The Dog's Working Behavior

How to Start   75

Equipment   79

       The Harness . . . The Lead . . . Stakes and Articles . . . Assistance

The Tracking Field   83
    Training Ground . . . Commands and Encourage-
    ment . . . Handling . . . Taut Lead
Incentive   91
    Creating Incentive in the Tracking Dog . . . The First
    Track . . . Reading the Dog . . . Restraint . . . The
    First Turn . . . The Value of Patience
Tracking Problems   107
    Individual Temperament . . . Reluctance to Work
    Ahead of the Handler . . . Reluctance to Pull in
    Harness . . . Food Reinforcement . . . Problems with
    Turns . . . Handler-Induced Problems . . . Wind-
    ing . . . Age of the Track . . . Tracklayers . . . Build-
    ing Confidence
Getting Ready for a Tracking Test   121
    Increasing the Difficulty . . . Unknown Tracks . . .
    Airborne Trails . . . Setting the Pace . . . Working
    Out Turns . . . Introducing New Challenges . . .
    Visual Trailing . . . Landmarks . . . Approaching
    Certification . . . Area of Test Tracks . . . At the
    Tracking Test
After the "T"   143
    Practical Tracking . . . Search and Rescue . . . Ad-
    vanced Tracking (TDX)
American Kennel Club Tracking Regulations   155
Conclusion   159
Bibliography   160

About the Author

IN the world of dog trainers, Wilson Davis has no peers. Justification for that admittedly bald and uncompromising statement crowds my memories of the years since we first met shortly after World War II.

At the time he was a Captain in the United States Marine Corps Reserve. The innovations which he developed in guard and scout dog tactics and training techniques were in themselves sufficiently successful to warrant the official acclaim he received from the Commanding General, 'Howling Mad' Smith.

Despite his combat-proved methods of training both dogs and men, it is doubtful that even he knew, then, how far his unique skill would take him, how many post-war military and civilian problems would be thrown in his lap for solution with the use of those war-developed talents. In addition to having engaged in virtually every aspect of dog training as a sport, he has trained dogs professionally for the Federal Government, the U.S. Marine Corps and with the Baltimore City Police Force where he retained the rank of Major—a title by which he is still known to his many friends and acquaintances in the Baltimore area.

Mr. Davis launched his lifetime of devotion to dog training when he joined the Dog Owners Training Club of Baltimore in 1936. Within a few years he became an instructor, produced an outline on basic obedience training which is still in use today, and was licensed as an obedience judge.

Not content with obedience alone, he branched out into conformation showing and field trial work, finishing many champions with obedience and field titles among his English Setters, Chesapeake Bay and Labrador Retrievers.

His first serious interest in working dogs began when he was appointed a regional director for Dogs for Defense shortly after the beginning of World War II. This was a volunteer group whose purpose was to recruit top quality dogs, mostly Doberman Pinschers and German Shepherds, for use by the Armed Forces as sentry dogs.

As the war progressed, Mr. Davis, along with a few other serious dog trainers, began to think in terms of military use of dogs in scout and messenger work. When the U.S. Marine Corps became seriously interested in the idea, he enlisted as an officer and was assigned to Camp LeJeune, N.C. with the War Dog Program.

This was the first of many serious challenges to be met by Mr. Davis in the course of his life in the field of dog training. It was his job to prove that the use of dogs was feasible and would work in the field of battle. He insisted upon going through the rigorous specialized training program of the Marine Scouts so that he would know exactly what was expected of the men and what might be expected of their dogs. He personally selected the men and dogs, determined their assignments to one another, and trained them to work as teams—mostly in advance scouting and mine detection.

Eventually he was assigned to the Pacific Theater and, as War Dog Officer for the Fleet Marine Force, Pacific, activated the War Dog Training and Administration Headquarters. He remained as C.O. of this unit for the duration of the war. The dogs proved invaluable in advance scout work. They were able to sense and detect more acutely than the most skillful man, and they were trained to communicate what they sensed to their handlers who, in turn, were trained to 'read' their dogs quickly and accurately, and act accordingly.

After the war Mr. Davis joined with a few friends in forming the Oriole Dog Training Club in Baltimore and resumed his activities as an obedience instructor, exhibitor and judge. Because of his outstanding reputation in the obedience fancy, the American Kennel Club twice appointed him to their Advisory Committees on revisions of the Obedience Regulations.

In the meantime the success of War Dogs in the Pacific had presented to Government and Military officials the possibilities of further uses of dogs, and Mr. Davis was consequently commissioned as a research consultant and advisor in forthcoming studies and texts aimed at the development of specialized dog training with emphasis on tracking and scent work.

Here is just one illustration of the sort of work he did in this capacity.

During certain phases of the missile testings at White Sands, N.M. several years ago, missiles were frequently detonated over the desert. Part of the success of these tests was contingent upon recovery of as many pieces of these missiles as possible for their re-assembly and study. The recovery of these fragments involved the use of several squads of men who searched the desert for days, even weeks, and the results, at best, often fell short of what was needed.

Mr. Davis believed that dogs could be used to recover these missile fragments at a tremendous saving of time and money and with better results. Two tests were set up to prove the idea. The first was a 'controlled' situation. An area 200×600 yds. was roped off and twelve grapefruit size metal balls, painted different colors, were placed within the area as they might be dropped from an exploded missile. Included in the paint was a chemical previously tested and proved to have a long-lasting, strongly identifiable scent to a dog. A team of men was sent to search the area and note, but not remove, as many of the balls as they could find. Twenty-seven minutes after starting, they had crossed the area and located seven balls. Wilson then took Dingo, a Weimaraner, into the area. Dingo found eleven balls, one of them elbow deep in ashes at the bottom of a crater with sides six feet high. Time—seven minutes, three seconds!

Next came the 'feasibility' test. A missile containing 600 metal balls was detonated over the desert. Of the 600 balls, 200 were painted yellow, 400 red. Half of the red balls were scented and marked as such for visual identification. The plan was to send a search crew out for two days to pick up as many yellow balls as they could find, after which, Mr. Davis and his associate were to come in with their dogs and find as many of the scented red balls as they could. The day they were supposed to fly out to White Sands, he got a call informing him that there had been some delays and he would be called when they were ready for his part in the test.

One week later, ten days after the detonation and immediately following one of the worst rain storms in the history of White Sands, the two men and their dogs were called in. In more than a week, working every day, a search crew of twenty men had found 176 of the 200 yellow balls. The two men and their dogs started out at 5:00 A.M. on the tenth day after detonation and had to quit at 1:00 P.M. due to extreme heat. In those seven hours they located visually 13 of the remaining yellow balls and 157 of the scented red balls! Needless to say, dogs were used thereafter on that job.

Mr. Davis is a continuing consultant to the Bio-Sensor Research Dept. of the Walter Reed Army Institute of Research. He has provided invaluable assistance to this unit's mission to develop, by selective breeding, a dog of superior intelligence, soundness and capability for possible use in many additional types of work.

Late in 1956 a series of articles appeared in a Baltimore newspaper on Scotland Yard, the last article of which concerned the Yard's use of dogs. Mr. Davis was not alone in his interest in this article. A week later a public statement was made by the Police Commissioner indicating his interest in the possibility of a similar use of dogs on the Baltimore City Police Force. A phone call by Mr. Davis to the Commissioner and several conferences later, the Baltimore City K-9 Corps was conceived.

Mr. Davis outlined a training program and selected two men from the force whom he knew to have done some obedience training. With his own dog and two carefully selected dogs for the other two men, they began their training. With only six months allowed them to prove the value of the idea, much of their training had to be done on the streets. Even in that short time the usefulness of the dogs was proven, and the Baltimore City Council approved the permanent establishment of the K-9 branch of the Police Force with Mr. Davis in charge.

After three years on the force, firmly establishing the K-9 Corps and its training program, he resigned to start his own K-9 Training Agency and Boarding Kennel north of Baltimore. It is here that we find him today. Although he has given up judging and rarely has time to train his own dogs for obedience and field competition, he is still very much a part of the obedience world. Mr. Davis is training director of the Oriole D.T.C., has his own training classes, and gives private instruction in all phases of training and in tracking. He has devised a format for an Advanced Tracking Test which he hopes to see recognized in the near future by the American Kennel Club for a T.D.X. obedience title.

Even the most cursory review of Wilson's life reveals that he has always leaned heavily toward practical applications of dog training. This has been the strongest thread in the fabric of his life with dogs. Even as a boy of 10, he trained his two dogs to work his paper route with him—he rolled the papers and the dogs, working opposite sides of the street, deposited them on the proper doorsteps. It was then, perhaps, that the stage was really set for his rich and rewarding life in the field of dog training.

To those of us who were privileged to train and learn training in the shadow of this man, his was a hand seldom gentle but always effective.

I have heard it said by his critics that Wilson Davis treats his dog pupils better than his human pupils. If that be true (and I have seen some evidence that it may be at least occasionally true), then the reason for it is that he has a greater understanding for dogs than for people.

A man of such unbending personal principles would be quite capable of having more basic respect for the uncomplicated loyalty of dogs than for the fathomless foibles of most humans.

Through the many years during which I studied under his guidance a close personal friendship developed.

My trust in him as a friend and my faith in him as an unexcelled dog trainer were put to the acid test one evening when he asked if I would agree to be part of a brief but dramatic demonstration of total control over a dog. Had I known beforehand just how dramatic the demonstration would be, perhaps a small second thought might have emerged.

At the time, besides his work in the obedience field, Mr. Davis was busily engaged in developing civilian guard dog training techniques and safe-use tactics as a consultant to the United States Government, a post he still holds. As might be expected, his own dog, a huge German Shepherd, was his prize pupil. I had petted, fed, romped with and even teased the dog during our numerous mutual training sessions. He was my friend, an affectionate face-licker who never failed to welcome me.

Then to the obvious horror of the selected few people watching, Wilson gave an inaudible attack signal to the dog. In the blink of an eye 100 pounds of bared fangs and pure muscle was launched through the air directly at me about shoulder high.

How fast can thoughts pass through the mind? Under such circumstances the answer is 'damn quick.' I had time for only two before it was all over but the applause. They were—HE WOULDN'T and THE HELL HE WOULDN'T!, meaning first, that my 100-pound, face-licking canine buddy wouldn't take me, followed instantly by the certain knowledge that he would.

But before either point was proved, Wilson gave a down command and Prince actually closed his mouth before his weight slammed me back against the wall and down on the floor in something of an untidy heap.

A bit winded by the impact, when I looked up, there was my 100-pound fuzzy buddy grinning his total friendliness as usual.

Lest the reader conclude that such demonstrations lightly attempted are dangerous, you are right. It is not recommended, not even by Wilson Davis. The saving feature, and another mark of this man's skill, was the fact that he had trained me as well as the dog and he knew I wouldn't move or try to pull away. He knew it and I suspect the dog knew it. But I didn't.

For most of the long, pleasant years of our friendship I have constantly badgered Wilson Davis to write a book on dog training, to put into words the basics of his unusual training methods which in my experience with dogs and trainers are outstandingly different, and more eminently successful than in many other more widely used methods.

Now at last he has done it. This treatise on the most complex of all dog training techniques, tracking, is in itself sufficient verification of my opening statement.

Writing is my profession and dog training is my avocation. From both viewpoints, Major Davis has done a superb job of work.

But then, that's the way he does everything . . .

Tom Cofield

Introduction

HISTORIANS record that the development of the man-dog relationship began in pre-historic times when nomadic man-tribes and packs of jackals established a primitive relationship of mutual dependence.

Jackals, the earliest ancestor of the dog, habitually followed man-tribes from camp to camp to forage for scraps of food left behind. At night they would encircle the camp, waiting for the tribe to move on the following day. Aware of the presence of the jackals, these primitive people soon realized that the scavenger packs lurking in the darkness around their camps were a protection against dangerous predators. At the approach of any such intruder, the jackals would set up a howl of warning to one another and men began to rely upon this alarm for their own protection.

The tribes found it to their advantage to deliberately leave food at abandoned camp sites and to drop pieces of food along the way as they moved from place to place to encourage the jackals to follow them. Thus, the stage was set for what today is the closest of all man-animal relationships—the companionship of man and dog.

True domestication undoubtedly took centuries to evolve from this primitive beginning, but it can be seen that the first step in the development of the man-dog relationship was man's exploitation, for his own protection, of the dog's natural abilities to detect danger and to track. It is ironic that today protection and tracking are regarded as advanced forms of dog training. They were, in fact, the two factors which first brought man and dog together.

Man has used the tracking dog throughout history. The earliest cave paintings depict dogs as companions of hunters. As civilization developed and hunting became a sport as well as a means of survival, dogs were bred for their hunting ability. They also were used for tracking down enemies and escaped slaves.

These uses of tracking dogs, have shown up in the history of every nation and civilization on earth. In present times tracking dogs may still be found as indispensible companions to the hunters of primitive tribes whose survival depends partially on wild game. Tracking dogs are the valued companions of sporting hunters; they are used militarily by many nations in espionage, scouting, messenger and defense work; they are used by law enforcement agencies in capturing criminals, locating stolen goods or caches of narcotics, and in search and rescue work.

As a competitive sport, tracking had its origins in Germany. The first writings on the subject of tracking and training a dog for this sort of work also came from Germany.

Tracking was first introduced into this country in the 1930's and has been a part of the obedience fancy since the adoption of the first American Kennel Club Obedience Regulations in 1936.

For the first nine months that these regulations were in effect, tracking was an 'exercise' in the requirements for earning a Utility title. Even after the regulations were amended, separating tracking from the Utility class, it was required that a dog had earned a tracking title before he could compete in the Utility class. These regulations remained in effect until 1947 when the Tracking title was separated from requirements having to do with any other obedience class and there has been no significant change in the requirements for earning a Tracking title since that time.

Since 1936 there has been only one major change in the conduct of Tracking tests. Until 1943 the manner in which the track-layer walked the track followed the British method. The track-layer walked the previously staked track to its end, dropped the article at the last stake and then retraced his steps, picking up the flags on the return trip. In 1943 this regulation was amended to require that the track-layer pick up the flags as he walked the track and leave the track by another route after dropping the article at the last flag.

The inclusion of tracking as part of the Utility class in this country served to demonstrate that most breeds could be successfully trained to track. This has been a continuing trend in the United States. The Tracking title has been earned by almost every breed of dog and is now recognized as attainable by anyone with any breed.

It is hoped that this book will offer a better understanding of the principles of tracking and an approach to training which will broaden the interest in this most satisfying of all forms of dog training.

* * * * *

My heartfelt thanks to Connie Spencer who has worked closely with me in putting this book together. Without her interest and ability to put my thoughts on paper, combined with her understanding of working dogs, this job would never have been done.

My gratitude also goes to Bob Lashbrook and Dave Boston for their cooperation and assistance in their official capacities with the United States Government.

I cannot overlook the boys who did most of the leg work in proving the principles of tracking—particularly Bobby Brooks, Tom Mark and Bob Lanning—and many others with whom I have worked over the years.

Thanks also to Carolyn Ensor and her three Weimaraners— "Gus", the father, and his two sons, "Rowdy" and "Foxy". All three track as though they had read the book!

And lastly, I cannot fail to mention two of my own dogs— "Barney", an English Setter who was my first tracking dog, and "Utah", a German Shepherd Dog who was possibly the greatest of all the tracking dogs I have trained.

L. W. D.

Fundamentals of Training

BEFORE beginning any type of dog training it is important to consider some of the basic principles involved. Regardless of the type of training in which you are interested, you must know what you wish to achieve. You must also understand what you must give of yourself and what you may expect of your dog.

Many people have satisfactory pets who only require training to overcome some annoying habit such as: refusal to come when called or jumping up on people. Others want more from training—a gun dog or field trial worker, an obedience competitor, protection dog or proficient tracker. Regardless of the reason for training, the results should produce a better pet and companion. The quality of the results will depend entirely upon the amount of time and effort you are willing to put into the training and the extent of your understanding of the dog's capabilities.

The first step in any type of dog training is the development of a means of communication which promotes mutual understanding between dog and handler. This requires willingness on the part of the trainer to accept the fact that he has as much to learn as the dog. You must observe the dog's natural behavior, his responses to sound and movement, his reactions to your typical behavior, particularly to your voice. For example, when you are displeased with your dog and speak harshly to him he may run from you, or he may lay his ears back and cower before you. He may creep toward you with quivering tail as if to beg forgiveness; or he may even stand defiantly in front of you as if to challenge your right to scold him. On the other hand, when you are pleased with him and speak to him affectionately or happily, he may react by nuzzling against you or relaxing into an attitude of complete self-satisfaction; he may go a little wild with joy, jumping against you or chasing about in random play. No matter what the dog's reaction to your tone-of-voice, expressions of pleasure or displeasure, once you have learned from his reactions that he understands whether or not you are pleased with him, you will have found the key to a means of communication with your dog. Your observations of his reactions will also give you a clue as to what will be necessary in your administration of correction and praise in future training.

All dog training is based on the dog's understanding of right and wrong. He learns the difference between right and wrong through your applications of correction and praise, and he looks primarily to your tone of voice for his understanding.

COMMON SENSE is an important element in communication and training and quite often produces better results than application of impersonal theory and technique. Consider, for instance, the elementary problem of housebreaking a puppy. It is commonly recommended to 'paper-train' a pup, on the theory that if he is taught to use only paper, eventually the paper may be removed and the dog will no longer make a mistake in the house. It frequently happens, however, that the dog still relieves himself after the paper has been removed and one must resort to other means. If you think about it you will realize the dog has actually been *trained to relieve himself in the house* by this method and, paper or no paper, he will return to the spot where he has been trained to go when necessary. It is much more logical to take the time and effort to exercise the puppy outdoors frequently, praise him when he relieves himself, and never give him an opportunity or excuse to do so in the house. Most dogs are naturally clean and will go as far as possible from where they eat or sleep to relieve themselves. When they understand that they will be taken out often enough to avoid discomfort, most

22

dogs will resist relieving themselves in the house in deference to their natural cleanliness.

This is only one example of the use of common sense in training. There are thousands of people with acceptable, well-trained house pets, who never read a book on dog training or attended an obedience training class. They simply use common sense by letting their dogs know when they are wrong and when they are right and turn them into the satisfactory companions they are.

Never hesitate to use common sense in training your dog. Regardless of what you are training him for or what method of training you choose to follow, you must approach each step in training on the basis of your own circumstances and your understanding of your own dog.

Timing is a vital factor in training. Correction or praise are meaningless with poor timing. Development of good timing calls for careful observation, learning to anticipate the dog's behavior and being prepared to make the most effective use of correction and immediate praise. Consider the annoying problem of the friendly dog who jumps up on everyone. This is often encouraged during puppyhood and rewarded with affection, making it a difficult habit to break. Pushing the dog away once his feet are up on you is rejection to him, not correction for the act of jumping up on you. You must anticipate the act and correct verbally and physically as the dog prepares to jump. Observation reveals that the dog's hindquarters dip to a slight crouch from which he can spring upwards. The moment you see that characteristic movement is the time for a correction. As the dog prepares to jump, put your hand straight out between you and the dog so that his muzzle will strike your palm as he springs upward. Don't raise your hand as if to pull away from or threaten the dog. This movement is more liable to encourage him to jump than it is to deter him. Let the dog come up against your palm. In effect, this causes the dog to correct himself as he is caught in the act of doing something you don't want him to do. Immediate praise, as he drops back to a sitting or standing position, will tell him he is right to stay down.

This brings us to the importance of observing your dog's physical behavior patterns. Careful study of your dog under a variety of circumstances will reveal certain behavior characteristics. There will be sounds or circumstances to which he reacts consistently. His reactions will show in the position or motion of his tail, head, ears, hindquarters, back, eyes or any combination of these. Learn to read these physical signs and captitalize on them in training. If you learn to recognize the signs of the dog's intentions, you can anticipate his errors and correct him at the most effective moment, as in the case of the jumping dog.

Anticipation is useful in giving effective praise as well. The dog may not be sure of what he should do in response to a new command and react hesitantly. If you can catch that first tentative response to a new command, immediate praise and encouragement will tell the dog he is right at the best possible time.

Consistency in training is essential. The dog must always understand exactly what you mean by your actions and tone of voice. This must apply to his behavior at all times, not just during periods of training. Inconsistency may result in a reverse of the desired effect. Consider, for instance, the problem of the shy, protective dog who is hostile to strangers. In attempting to overcome this, people often try to calm the dog, reassure him that the other person is all right. What they don't realize is that they are, in effect, *praising* the dog for his hostility by petting him and telling him, "It's all right, boy, it's all right." The dog still feels the hostility, and reassuring words and petting encourage his attitude as he feels he is being praised for it. In such a case, a sharp correction, consistent with the way he has been corrected for other misbehavior, will tell him he is wrong. The dog must know when he is right or wrong. He will understand only through consistent, clear-cut applications of correction and praise.

Understanding is the sole purpose of communication in training. It can only be achieved through tone of voice and inflection. These are difficult to inject into monosyllabic words. In practical training whether it is a command, a correction or praise, multiple-word phrases offer opportunity for a much wider range of expression. Such phrases afford the handler more natural and meaningful utterance of his honest intent or feeling. This enhances the dog's understanding of what is required of him.

Let us say, for example, that you have a problem with a dog who charges through the door every time you open it, causing you considerable annoyance. It might seem logical to control the situation by telling the dog to stay before opening the door, and releasing

24

him after you have passed through. Even though he obeys each time you give him a formal command to stay, will he really understand that it annoys you to have him crowd you in the doorway and that he is *never* to do so? This is not a training problem to be solved or handled like an 'exercise'. It is a practical behavior problem which can more effectively be solved by natural-phrase communication in place of formal, one-word commands. Let the dog know the full extent of your annoyance. Turn on him just as he is about to lunge through the doorway. Look him in the eye and shake your finger or fist at him. Raise your voice with all the irritation you really feel and say, "Now, you *stay* there until I get through that door!" From that short tirade the dog will respond to your tone of voice and understand your honest displeasure. It will take only a few such encounters to bring him to the point where he will gladly stop and wait for you to go through the door first, with no command necessary, just to avoid your displeasure. He must also understand your satisfaction with his improved behavior. Once you are through the door, you should say something like, "That's it! Come on now, let's go!"

This use of informal-phrase communication may be applied to making verbal corrections, in obedience training as well. NO is probably the most grossly over-used word in dog training. Alone, it is not really a correction. It only tells the dog to "stop". Any short, sharp word or unpleasant throaty or nasal sound would do well. Let us say you have a problem with a whining dog. You NO and the dog stops whining. As soon as you turn your attention elsewhere, he begins to whine again. He stops when you say NO, but the effect only lasts as long as your attention is on the dog. Eventually he may learn through constant repetition of the word NO that he should *never* whine, but he will learn more quickly and effectively if you communicate your displeasure through more expressive verbal communication. You might tell him to "Stop that", "Now you stop that right now!", "Shut up!", "Knock it off!", or any natural expression which really conveys your irritation. The dog will soon realize, through understanding your tone of voice, that whining is unforgivable at any time.

In this informal approach to communication with the dog, praise is vital and must never be neglected. Praise is more than just a way of letting the dog know he is right. It enhances his willingness

25

to learn and work. When praise is used properly it serves to double the effectiveness of correction. If you have been working on an obedience exercise which has proven difficult for both you and the dog, you will be exceptionally pleased the first time he does it right. He should experience the same feeling of "success at last" that you do and should be allowed to share your satisfaction with the resolution of the problem. If you give him a perfunctory pat on the head and mumble "good boy", you deprive the dog of the sense of accomplishment you feel. If, on the other hand, you tell him, with honest enthusiasm, "*That's* it! Now you've got it! Good boy!", he will understand the degree of your pleasure and be eager to comply in future practice of the exercise.

In considering these examples of basic practical training problems, it can be seen that communication is more than teaching the dog words and response to words. Communication is a matter of mutual understanding. You have ways of knowing when a dog's attitude is negative and when it is positive. Give him the benefit of equal understanding. Let him know the full measure of your pleasure and displeasure.

Single words such as are traditionally used in obedience training evoke automatic response through repetition and training, but little understanding. There is no reason why you should not communicate naturally and informally with your dog in practice of exercises as well as in practical training. Teach him the formal commands, condition him to brief correction and praise, but don't lose touch with the dog by allowing yourself to be limited to artificial terminology. A dog *learns* by repetition of commands, signals and physical guidance with correction and praise. He *understands* through honest, natural communication of his handler-trainer.

The use of correction and praise in training must have the same purpose and achieve the same results as verbal instruction of another person. When you teach a person to do something, you explain or describe what he is to do. When he does it wrong, you tell him what his mistakes were, and when he performs correctly you tell him he is right. The same should apply to training a dog.

Obedience training is pointless if it is not applied daily toward the development of a dog who understands what is acceptable and what is not. If obedience training is to have a positive effect upon the dog's daily behavior it must be regarded as part of or an extension of practical training. Natural-talk communication is necesssary to give meaning to training and control.

From the simplest exercise to the most complex ring or field work, correction and praise are the basis of communication with a dog in training. Correction lets the dog know he is wrong and praise lets him know he is right. Expressions of correction and praise must be natural and they must be used honestly in expressing pleasure or displeasure. The dog cannot understand the meanings of words, but he does respond to inflection and tone of voice. Therefore, any phrase of expression uttered sharply or harshly will mean "wrong", and any phrase of expression uttered in a reassuring or enthusiastic tone of voice will mean "right".

Nagging is one of the worst and most common mistakes made in dog training. It is the result of improper application of commands and corrections. Monotonous repetition of commands uttered in a nonauthoritative tone of voice is nagging. Tugging on the collar which merely pulls the dog instead of correcting him amounts to nagging. A command is not a command unless it is backed up with an authoritative tone of voice, and physical guidance when necessary. A correction is not a correction unless it really tells the dog he is wrong and shows him how he is wrong. A dog that is nagged in training learns very little and soon becomes bored and inattentive. This can spell disaster to a training program since a dog's alertness and will to learn are so vitally important to success.

Avoid excessive use of, or dependence upon the word NO. NO is best used when you can anticipate the dog about to do something wrong. If you are heeling your dog, for instance, and his attention is drawn to another dog barking, a quick NO before he is actually distracted from the heel position will alert his attention back to you. Then a reassuring phrase such as, "That's it, now you pay attention to me", as you continue walking, will keep his attention on you and let him know he is right.

One of the hardest jobs an obedience instructor has is impressing upon human students the importance of praise. People are often inclined to neglect praise until perfection is attained. A dog does not understand the ultimate aim of each step in training and, even though his performance may be far short of perfection, he must be praised for every step in the right direction. For example, the three steps in teaching a dog to sit straight at heel are: sit, at heel, and straight. The first time the dog sits on command, regardless of where or how, he must be praised. As you progress and the dog sits at heel, even though he sits crookedly, he must be praised. Each time he sits a little straighter or more quickly than the time before, he must be praised.

In moving exercises such as heeling and the recall, praise may be given through encouragement as the dog is working. A few pleasant words from time to time as you are heeling will let the dog know he is pleasing you by walking at your side and will cause him to enjoy it. Informal encouragement as the dog moves toward you when he is learning the recall will tell him he is right and make him want to come to you for praise.

Correction and praise are also applied by physical means—one short, sharp jerk on the slip-chain collar to tell the dog he is wrong, and a pat on the head or shoulder to tell him he is right. Physical correction and praise should always be accompanied by verbal correction and praise. This serves to double the effectiveness of your communication of right and wrong. The consistent combined use of verbal and physical communication in early training also will assure understanding on the part of the dog should circumstances require use of either type of communication alone in practical situations or later training.

Neither correction nor praise should be over-done. Over-correcting may effect the dog as punishment and destroy his willingness to learn and eagerness to please. Too much exuberance in giving praise may destroy the control necessary in a training session, causing the dog to forget what the praise was for.

Correction must *always* be followed immediately by praise whether or not the situation seems to warrant it. Even if the dog's reaction to a collar correction is nothing more than an involuntary one (as when you bring a lagging heeler into position by a sharp jerk on the collar), he must be praised so that he associates the correction with a change from wrong to right. Correction alone is meaningless to a dog in the learning process. When you teach a child what is "wrong", you also teach him what is right. In teaching a dog the same training principle exists. In order to teach him what is wrong you correct, and in order to teach him what is right you praise. To make this training principle work, it is imperative that correction always be balanced with praise.

Severity of correction should be determined by the type and size of the dog and his individual temperament. One would hardly apply the same degree of physical correction to a Toy Poodle as to a German Shepherd. Neither would one apply the same degree of physical or verbal correction to a dog who is eager to please, as to an inattentive or stubborn dog. In determining the degree of severity of correction to be used, bear in mind the importance of maintaining a sound balance between correction and praise. If you must be very stern with your dog, you must be most lavish when you praise him. If your dog responds best to a lesser degree of severity, praise must be equally conservative. Such a balance of emphasis between correction and praise will greatly enhance the dog's understanding of both right and wrong.

There is no mystique in successful training and handling of a dog. People often are awed by someone who seems to have a "gift" with animals. It is true that some people have a greater aptitude than others for working with animals, but this aptitude is born of greater interest, application of observation and common sense, making the effort to understand and learn from the dog, and willingness to temper the attitude of total human superiority.

Children frequently are successful in training their dogs to do quite complicated "tricks". We can learn something from watching such children. They teach their dogs in much the same manner as they have been taught. They talk to their dogs with complete lack of sophistication or self-consciousness, explaining what they want as they manipulate their dogs physically to show them what they should do. They get frustrated and give up for a while and then go back to it again. They are persistent and they are consistent. They are filled with love and pride once they have attained their goal, and they unashamedly demonstrate that love and pride to their dogs. They are natural and uninhibited in their relationships with their dogs and they are rewarded with devotion and obedience. That is what communication in dog training is all about.

Basic Control Exercises

I T is essential that a dog have some basic obedience training before venturing into tracking. A tracking dog must be under control at all times. Successful training for tracking can only be achieved if control and acceptance of training have been established through teaching basic exercises. Since it would constitute a digression from the main purpose of this book, not all of the exercises normally included in basic obedience training are included here. The following is an outline of the exercises recommended as essential to basic control, and a logical method of teaching them.

In obedience training you have three tools with which to work—verbal communication, physical control and body motion. Proper use of these tools will determine much of the success of your training program.

The collar must never be pulled tight and the lead must never be held taut. Both must be slack to assure that good, clear-cut corrections may be made when necessary. The lead should never be used to drag the dog or to hold him in restraint.

It will facilitate early training if you use both signal and command in teaching a new exercise. Consistent use of a signal with

31

The dog is sitting correctly at heel and is attentive to the handler.

each command will tend to hold the dog's attention and will lend emphasis to the verbal command. It will be shown that signals frequently are part of body motion to show the dog what you expect of him in response to a new command. If commands and signals are used together consistently, the transition from use of both to use of one or the other should present no problem once the dog is thoroughly trained.

Never wait for the dog to obey a command. Never coax him with ineffective repetitions of a command. When you do not get a prompt response to a command, repeat the command once in a reprimanding tone of voice and accompany it with a sharp collar correction, followed immediately by praise. A dog must learn not only the exercises, he must also learn that you expect immediate obedience to every command. This is the only way to establish control. If you wait for the dog, you allow *him* to control the situation which defeats the whole purpose of training.

Proper emphasis on the command is very important to the success of teaching a new exercise. For this reason, use of the dog's name is not recommended for inexperienced handlers who usually use a dog's name incorrectly, placing more emphasis on the name than on the command. They either use the name after the command or say the name more loudly than the command. In either case, the greater emphasis is placed on the name. Corrrectly used, the dog's name alerts his attention just before a command is given. Incorrectly used, it distracts him from attention to the command. Since you want *all* vocal emphasis on the command when teaching a new exercise, it is better not to use the dog's name at all than to use it incorrectly. Once the dog knows the exercise, his name may be used to get his attention just before giving the command.

First, the dog must be taught to heel. This essentially means position to him, whether or not the handler is in motion. When you walk, your dog walks at heel on your left side. When you stop, your dog sits at heel. In teaching a dog to heel, body motion is an important tool. If you consistently move the same way, starting and stopping on the same foot, the dog will soon learn to recognize these body motions as signals to which he will respond automatically.

To teach the command to "heel", start with the dog sitting at

33

The handler is shown testing the lead for the proper amount of slack.

your left side, the lead held slack in your right hand. The left hand should be free to grasp the lead for quick corrections and for giving praise. The correct amount of slack in the lead may be determined by swinging the right arm straight out to your side. The lead should become taut when your arm is raised to about a 45° angle from your body.

Give the command to "heel", swing your left arm forward as a signal and step out on your left foot. If the dog does not respond, grasp the lead with the left hand close to the collar, repeat the command once, simultaneously giving a sharp jerk on the lead as you step forward again. Remove your left hand from the lead as soon as the dog is in motion and give him a rewarding pat and a few words of praise or encouragement. If the dog forges ahead, give a sharp corrective jerk on the lead and a reprimanding "heel" command, then praise him to tell him he is right. In jerking the lead, it is important that the left arm swing from the shoulder, not the elbow, so the motion of the left arm and hand becomes a signal and shows the dog where he should be. With repetition of this routine, the dog will learn to respond to a single verbal command to "heel", as well as to hand signals.

When you come to a halt, you want the dog to sit automatically and instantly at heel. Before stopping, take up the slack in the lead, moving your right hand close to the collar. This will give you better control as you come to a quick halt. Check the dog's forward motion with an upward tug on the lead and press his hindquarters down with your left hand, at the same time giving the command to "sit". In pressing the dog's hindquarters down, use your thumb and fore-finger rather than the flat of your hand. A quick, sharp squeeze above the hips will cause the dog to yield with less resistance than he might exert under pressure of the flat of your hand. All actions and commands should be executed smoothly and quickly so that the dog does not become confused or feel that he is engaged in a struggle. As soon as the dog sits, all hand and collar pressure must be promptly released and the dog praised. This exercise should be repeated in its entirety until it is virtually impossible to touch the dog's hindquarters before he sits. If you are consistent in teaching this exercise, the dog will shortly drop to an automatic sit, with no verbal or physical guidance, as soon as your left foot comes to rest when you halt.

The next step in training is teaching the dog to "stay". This exercise offers an excellent illustration of proper use of body motion in training, as well as the importance of consistency. Just as you conditioned the dog to move forward when you lead off with your left foot in heeling, it now is important that you make a point of NOT stepping away with your left foot when leaving the dog on a stay. Remember that the dog understands signals and body motion. If you now give him an unfamiliar command to "stay", and step forward on your left foot (your body motion is a signal to "heel") you will be contradicting yourself and confusing your dog.

With the dog sitting at heel, switch the lead to the left hand, place the open palm of your right hand in front of his face and give the command to "stay". Step forward on your right foot and pivot to a position facing the dog. The lead is switched from the right to the left hand because you want the dog conditioned to the use of the right hand for all signals except heeling. In early stages of teaching the dog to stay, stand immediately in front of and facing him so as to be close enough to make a correction when necessary. As he begins to understand what is required of him, gradually increase the distance between you and the dog until he will stay in position at the full length of the lead. Each time you work on this, the dog must remain sitting until you return to the heel position by walking around him counterclockwise and coming to a halt by his right side.

If the dog starts to get up or lie down, check him immediately with a sharp NO. Simultaneously, with a collar correction, position him on the original spot facing the same direction and repeat the command to "stay". Since you want the correction to apply only to the dog's failure to stay, do not repeat the command to "sit" unless he has moved from the original spot.

When the dog will stay for several minutes at the full length of the lead, he should be tested by applying a gentle, steady pulling on the lead. A dog who is reliable on stays will physically resist considerable pulling on the lead. When testing the dog this way, take care not to jerk the lead so that he does not feel he is being corrected. This is more than a simple test—it is part of the training. The need for correction when the dog is six feet away cannot be dealt with as quickly as it should be. Pulling on the lead not only

The dog is heeling perfectly alongside his handler.

Preparing to halt.

Placing the dog in the proper sitting position.

Preparing to leave the dog on a "stay".

The dog is in the proper "sit-stay" position on leash.

The handler is testing the dog for reliability on the "sit-stay".

tests the dog's reliability on stays, it also creates an opportunity for correction at the most effective moment if he does yield to the pulling. Before the dog actually gets up, you will feel a slight slackening in the lead as he prepares to "break". The instant you feel that slackening, check the dog's intention with a sharp NO, followed by a repeat of the command to "stay".

It is advisable to practice stays in the presence of distractions such as crowds of moving people, other animals or anything else which might cause the dog to break a stay. This will provide additional opportunities for corrections and praise which are so vital in training.

When the dog will stay in the sit position, it is time to teach him to "down". Put the dog on a sit-stay and stand close in front of him, holding the lead in your left hand. As you give the command to "down", raise your right arm and bring it down in a straight sweeping motion as a corresponding signal. Bring your fingertips down firmly on the withers (between the shoulder blades) at the end of the armswing and press the dog down. A slight downward pull with the left hand on the lead, close to the collar, will assist in this. The dog must always go down when your fingertips press on his withers so that he thoroughly understands the meaning of this particular physical contact.

This frequently is a difficult exercise to teach since it is not uncommon to encounter resistance on the part of the dog. Wrestling with him must be avoided since this will only increase his resistance and teach him nothing. The problem of resistance may be overcome in the following manner. As the dog resists the pressure of your right hand on his withers, drop the lead and reach behind his right foreleg with your left hand. Grasp his left foreleg and scoop both legs out from under him, guiding him down with continuing pressure of your right hand on his withers. When scooping the dog's legs out from under him, raise them slightly and bring them forward so that the dog goes down in a comfortable, stretched out position. This must be done quickly and smoothly, with only a single repeat of the command, followed immediately by release and praise. Do not hold the dog down. If he gets up right away, go through the entire procedure until the dog understands that he is to stay in that position until you release him. Take care not to use roughness in teaching this exercise. If the dog is knocked down or thrown

Signalling the "down".

The dog is being placed in the down position.

At times it is necessary to bring the dog's front legs out in front of him when teaching the "down" position.

off balance it will only increase his resistance and teach him nothing more than wrestling will.

In order to facilitate teaching the down, you may train the dog to come up to a sit from the down position. Standing directly in front of the dog, put him down by command and signal, then give him the command to "sit". Simultaneously swing your right arm upward as a signal, tapping him smartly under the chin with your fingertips to emphasize the command signal. You may assist the dog into a sit position with an upward jerk on the lead with your left hand.

Once the dog will drop automatically into the down position on command and signal, give the command and signal to stay as in the sit-stay exercise. Circle around the dog to the heel position before releasing him. The dog should not sit up as you come to the heel position until you give him the command to do so. Vary the length of time you stand at heel in practicing this exercise so the dog understands that he must wait for your command to sit. You may also test the dog for reliability on the down-stay by pulling on the lead in the same manner you tested him on the sit-stay.

When the dog will stay reliably in both sit and down positions, he is ready for the "recall". With the dog on a sit-stay, stand at the end of the lead, give the command "come", and with your right arm make a full-sweeping, beckoning motion. Simultaneously give a sharp jerk on the lead to start the dog in motion toward you. As soon as the dog starts toward you he must be liberally praised and encouraged to keep coming. If he seems unsure or reluctant, give another corrective jerk on the lead, repeat the command and take a few steps backward. Encourage him. Keep his attention on you. Let him know that it pleases you to have him come to you. As he moves forward, encourage him to a position in front of you and tell him to sit. The dog may and should be corrected for not coming, but the instant he starts in your direction, he is doing what you want, and praise at this point is essential.

The lead must only be used for correction. It must not be used to pull or guide the dog in any way. If the dog starts moving off to the side or becomes interested in something other than coming to you, a sharp jerk on the lead will bring his attention and direction back to you more effectively than if you drag him in.

The recall is the most important of all control exercises. It is

Signalling the dog to sit from the "down" position.

The dog is being given the "stay" command while in the "down" position.

The dog returns to the handler after receiving the command to "come". This is known as the "recall".

the basis of all off-lead control, in everyday life as well as in various types of obedience training. Correction and praise are of primary importance in teaching the recall since the dog must be absolutely dependable in his response to the command to "come". No corrections should be made for anything other than failure to come. For instance, if the dog is corrected for failure to sit straight during early stages of teaching the recall, he is liable to think he is being corrected for coming. He must be firmly corrected for every sign of inattention to the command, and he must be assured of the reward of honest praise for his direct and instant response to the command.

People often are misled into believing that they have successfully trained their dogs to do the recall with little or no trouble because their dogs have responded eagerly from the start. These same dogs, however, will often prove to be undependable under practical, everyday conditions. Their eager response in training and under controlled conditions may have left little opportunity for correction. They cannot actually be said to have been *trained* to do the recall. They do it because they like to, but are just as liable *not* to do it when they don't want to. To eliminate this eventuality you must create situations in training which will cause the dog to make errors, giving you the opportunity for firm correction. You will need to work with a longer lead to give you more working room. A piece of clothesline or nylon cord, 15–20 ft. long will do. Have someone else stand nearby, put the dog on a sit-stay, go to the end of the line and face him. Just after you give the command to "come" and the dog has started toward you, have the other person call the dog. As soon as his attention is drawn to the other person, give him a very sharp correction with the lead and a harsh single repeat of the command, followed by praise and encouragement as he recovers and comes toward you.

You might also practice in areas where there are other animals or children at play. Use any device you can to make the dog make a mistake in practicing the recall, giving you frequent reason to correct him. The more conscientiously you pursue this approach to teaching the recall, the more dependable your dog will be. Your reward will be well worth the effort when you know that you have a dog who will come instantly, under *any* circumstances, when he is called.

47

Before seeking or creating opportunities for correction, be certain the dog understands what his response to the command should be. Be especially attentive to the importance of giving praise proportionate to each correction.

Once the dog responds dependably to the "come" command he may be trained to sit correctly in front of you. The return-to-heel or finish of the recall exercise is taught separately, and only after the dog knows the recall itself.

The dog may return to heel in either of two ways. He may swing around to the left into the heel position or pass to your right and circle behind you to the heel position on the left.

To teach the former, hold the lead in your left hand, close to the collar. Give the command to "heel" and a jerk on the lead as you take one step backward. As the dog starts to pass on your left, move forward one step, repeating the command to "heel" and the collar correction. This will bring the dog around to the heel position. Then give the command to sit. To teach the alternate method, hold the shortened lead in your right hand. Give the heel command as you step back and, with a jerk on the lead, bring the dog around your right side. Exchange the lead from the right to the left hand behind your back. Step forward and, with another jerk on the lead, bring the dog around to the heel position where you will have him sit. The body motions of stepping backward and forward are only to facilitate the training and should be eliminated as soon as the dog understands what is expected of him. Because of the relative complexity of teaching this exercise, it is necessary to use three commands as well as extra body motion—"heel"—step back, "heel"—step forward, "sit". When the dog understands what is required of him, eliminate all body motion. Return to use of a slack lead so that the collar corrections may be made if the dog does not respond to a single command to "heel".

These are the basic control exercises which constitute the minimum training any dog should have before starting on tracking.

Retrieving is not a necessary prerequisite for teaching practical tracking. It is, however, very useful in training for an A.K.C. tracking test where a relatively small article must be designated by the dog to complete the test successfully. A dog trained to retrieve may enjoy the advantage of additional incentive in tracking once he learns that he will retrieve an article at the end of every track.

Here the dog is shown sitting correctly in front of the handler.

Step one of teaching the dog to heel by swinging him around to the handler's left.

Step two brings him in closer.

Step three has the dog in proper position.

The dog is in the correct position prior to returning to heel.

Retrieving is a relatively simple exercise when taught properly. The mistake most commonly made in teaching the retrieve is *forcing* the dog to take or pick up a specific article such as a dumbbell. Although the dog eventually will be required to pick up specific articles, this should not be introduced until after he is proficient at retrieving random articles. Force retrieving should not be necessary for an average, sound dog. It is a training method apart which should not be attempted except under direction of an experienced instructor.

Play retrieving is very effective as long as it remains a game in which the dog is encouraged to go after a tossed object. Retrieving is natural to a sound, stable dog. Any healthy puppy will chase a moving object. When he knows he will be praised and the object will be thrown for him to chase again when he returns it to his handler, he will do so for pure love of the game. This has been proven in the Army Bio-Sensor Research program where many puppies of various breeds retrieve at the age of seven weeks. Once the retrieving game is well established, the formalities of obedience commands may be worked in gradually and specific articles introduced as objects of the chase. Play retrieving may be introduced any time before or during other training, but the formalities of doing it as an exercise must not be introduced until after the dog has been trained to do the recall.

There are certain aspects of this approach to training which are of sufficient importance that they must be re-emphasized.

Look for and welcome situations requiring corrections in training and practice. Take full advantage of them to reinforce your training. For example, if your dog is heeling wide, exaggerate his error by stepping away from him rather than closer to him, thereby creating the opportunity for a more effective correction. If the dog is crowding you, walk into him rather than away from him. If he is lagging, speed up rather than slow down. If he is forging, slow down rather than speed up. Never adapt yourself to the dog in order to compensate for a mistake on his part. The dog must make mistakes and be corrected for them in order to learn. Bear in mind the importance of praise immediately following every correction. A balanced pattern of meaningful correction followed by rewarding praise strengthens the dog's understanding of what is required of him.

Step one of teaching the return to heel involves having
the dog going around behind the handler.

Step two of teaching the dog to heel
by going around behind the handler.

Step three in teaching the return to heel—the dog should be sitting at the handler's left at the end of the exercise.

By our intellectual standards, the dog has a relatively simple mind and learns through a process of doing exercises over and over again. Repetition must be wisely handled in training. In repeating commands and signals, care must be taken that they be single repetitions accompanied by single corrections, as needed, in the course of practicing an entire exercise. Constant repetition of commands which amount to nagging, or signals which amount to nothing more than random arm-wavings, soon lose all effectiveness and meaning to the dog. Practice of any exercise should consist of a regularly followed series of single commands, signals and body motions, with corrections when necessary. This, of course, applies to practice of formal exercises and is by no means meant to contradict the informal approach to practical training and communication recommended earlier. Practice sessions should last no more than 15 to 20 minutes and should include a variety of exercises. These sessions should be conducted in good humor and cut short if you feel you are losing patience.

Consistency is of vital importance in training. If you teach an exercise one way today and another way tomorrow, or neglect to use the same command and signal for any single act you are teaching, the dog will become confused. Overcoming such confusion will take much longer than if you are absolutely consistent right from the beginning.

It will be noted that no recommendation is made for the use of mechanical devices in any aspect of training. To train the average dog it is not necessary to use anything other than the collar and lead, your voice, hands and body motion. Mechanical devices or other "gimmicks" may be useful in handling certain problem dogs, but they confuse the real purpose of training a sound, stable dog. Part of the reason for training is the establishment of communication with the dog as a means of control. Since you must eventually rely solely upon verbal commands and signals, it is logical to start that way and rely upon them during all training. The use of unnecessary mechanical devices often tends to create other training problems as the dog must eventually learn to work without them.

Any basic training program must be logically planned and followed. Each exercise must have as its foundation what has been taught previously. Each exercise must lead directly into what is to be taught next. This approach produces a smooth progression of training which is less confusing to the dog and enhances his willingness to learn.

In a tracking dog you want a companion who accepts control as a natural way of life, a dog who has a well-developed will to please, to learn and to work. These are qualities which may only be developed through patient and intelligent basic training.

The Natural Basis
of Tracking

IT is a known fact that every dog is endowed by nature with the ability to follow a trail. It is also a known fact that it is more difficult for a dog to track under some conditions than it is under others. Once the fact is accepted that the dog *can* track, regardless of circumstances, the reason for one set of conditions being difficult and another easy becomes relatively unimportant. It must be understood and accepted that it is the dog and the dog alone who knows *how* he tracks.

There are three simple facts on which all tracking is based. These facts are based upon conclusions arrived at during seventeen years of continuing research on scent and tracking conducted by the U.S. Government. Every known theory, no matter what its source or how unlikely it seemed, was tested and proved, disproved or relegated to the realm of continuing speculation. In this research work conclusions were arrived at only after 100 tests were run on each study with 90% consistency of results.

Experience has demonstrated that the few concrete facts which emerged from this research are sufficient foundation for training a dog in tracking. Experience has also shown that chances of success increase when theory and speculation are not allowed to interfere with training a dog.

First, a tracking dog follows a trail left on the ground by a person walking over the terrain. Second, the dog can follow an airborne trail left in the immediate atmosphere and carried down-wind to be deposited on the ground or higher objects. Third, the dog is able to distinguish between individuals.

It will be noted that in referring to the ground and airborne trails the word "scent" is not used. There will be times when this word must be used for lack of a more definitive term, but it must be borne in mind that man's conception of scent is entirely different from what it is to the dog. When we think of scent we naturally think of "smell"; and when we think of the dog's ability to follow a trail by scent we tend to measure that ability against our own sense of smell.

We know that a blind-folded man would be unable to distinguish by scent the freshly washed hand of his own mother from that of a stranger. We also know that a dog is able to distinguish the specific scent of any individual, stranger or not. From this it might seem logical to assume that the dog simply has a sharper sense of smell than man. But let us take this a step further. If a skunk sprays your prize rose bush, you will be unable to smell the roses. If the assumption that the dog's sense of smell is simply keener than ours is correct, certainly the odor of skunk would obliterate any other odor even more for him than it does for you. This is not true. Tests have been made with skunk odor, among many others, and it has been proven that a dog trained in scent work is capable of correctly designating a particular article by scent from among a number of articles, all of which have been sprayed by a skunk. We must therefore conclude that the dog's ability to discern scent is something unique to him and may not be regarded as similar to our own sense of smell. We must also then accept the fact that when the dog is tracking, he is following a trail which he alone recognizes in a way which he alone understands.

A trained tracking dog will follow either the ground trail or the airborne trail, depending upon which is easier under prevailing circumstances or conditions. He is always aware of the presence

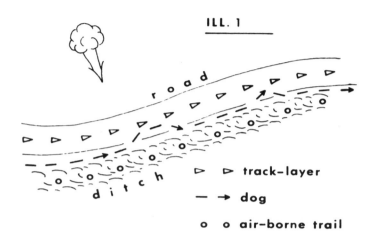

ILL. 1

r o a d

d i t c h

▷　▷ track-layer

— → dog

o　o air-borne trail

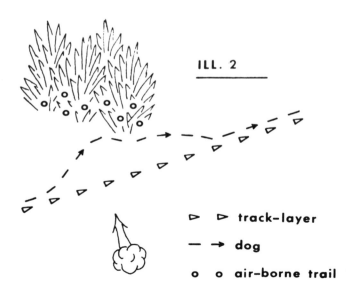

ILL. 2

▷　▷ track-layer

— → dog

o　o air-borne trail

of both trails and when he is following one he will frequently check the other. He also will change from one to the other as changes in conditions occur which alter the favorability of one trail over the other.

If the track-layer walks down a hard-surfaced road, the ground trail will not be as strong as when he walks across a grassy area. In such a case, the dog will follow the airborne trail. If the wind is blowing across the road and there is a ditch alongside (Ill. 1), the airborne trail will drift and settle there and the dog will follow the ditch where the airborne trail is concentrated. His awareness of the presence of both trails will prompt him to return from time to time to check the ground trail down the middle of the road. When the track-layer turns off the road to cross a field, the dog will resume following the easier ground trail. In addition to its tendency to settle in low spots, the airborne trail will collect on higher objects such as bushes or hedgerows near the path of the track-layer. As the dog follows a ground trail he will occasionally check the airborne trail (Ill. 2) where it has collected on such nearby higher or denser objects.

It is not necessary to understand the exact nature of the ground trail or the airborne trail in order to know that the dog can and will follow them. We may speculate indefinitely on whether the ground trail is recognized by the dog as crushed vegetation, disturbed earth or a scent impressed upon the surface by the shoes of the track-layer, and we will not determine anything which will increase our understanding of just what the trail is to the dog. We may theorize at length about the airborne trail, its intensity, its movement or rate of dissipation, and we will not alter the fact that it is there and the dog recognizes and follows it. This has been proven through observation and study of the consistent working patterns of many trained tracking dogs under a variety of extreme testing conditions.

It has been proven that the dog is able to distinguish between individuals, not only between persons known to him, but between strangers as well. In observing this capability we must conclude that each individual possesses, as part of his chemical anatomy, some characteristic unique to him which is constant and cannot be disguised or eliminated.

From chemical and biological research it has been learned that there exists a skin lubricant called *sebum* which meets these specifications. Experiments have shown that sebum reproduces so rapidly that even thorough antiseptic scrubbing can remove it from the surface of the skin for only a matter of seconds. One of the most conclusive experiments made in scent research was conducted to test the enduring qualities of sebum, as well as its indisputably individual character. A few years before the actual test, samples of sebum were chemically extracted, mostly from hair clippings, from several individuals and from various parts of the country. These samples were "canned" in a variety of preservatives such as formaldehyde, alcohol, etc. Just prior to the test, articles were obtained which had been recently handled by the same individuals from whom the sebum samples had been taken. These articles were used to give the scent to the dogs. A few drops of each of the preserved sebum samples were put onto otherwise sterile articles and it was the task of the dogs to match the articles. Despite the age of the sebum and the presence of some overwhelming preservative odors, the dogs did not fail in a single instance to accurately and decisively match each man-scented article with the corresponding article scented with the preserved sebum.

This and other conclusive experiments have clearly proven that every individual has a constant characteristic which is recognizable to a dog and by which he is able to distinguish between individuals.

We have now established the three fundamental facts upon which all tracking is based—the presence of a ground trail, the presence of an airborne trail and the presence of an individual characteristic in every person. Once you accept these, along with the fact that the dog is uniquely and consistently capable of recognizing them, you have all the foundation of knowledge to proceed in tracking.

In the course of establishing these principles of tracking, numerous observations have been made of how a tracking dog works. From these observations several pertinent conclusions have been drawn, most of which have to do with discarding many popularly-held ideas about such factors as contamination and interference.

It is often thought, even accepted as fact, that a trail can be obliterated or changed, deliberately or by chance, to the extent that it is impossible for a dog to follow it. One aim of many Government experiments was to find a way of consistently and decisively obliterating a trail to defeat the tracking dog. In these tests trails were laid through "impossible" terrain, changed from grassy areas to hard-surfaced roads and back again. Large fields were sprayed with gasoline and burned after tracks were laid through them. Fields were deep-plowed after track-layers had crossed them. Foreign odors, organic and inorganic, attractive and repelling, were introduced across and on top of previously laid tracks. Track-layers were picked up in cars and driven several hundred yards where they continued the tracks, or they removed their shoes along the trail, replaced them with a sterilized pair and continued the track. Track-layers entered rivers, swam downstream under water with snorkels and emerged on the opposite banks to continue the tracks. None of these tactics or devices consistently defeated the trained tracking dogs used in these tests. Had any of these experiments succeeded in demonstrating a sure way to defeat all the dogs, we would have come a long way in learning just how they track. We also would have gained a valuable defensive weapon since it is as useful militarily to be able to defeat a dog working against us as to have a dog working reliably for us.

Not all of the dogs "passed" all of the tests. Their failures taught us, among other things, some valuable lessons about handling a tracking dog. Most of the dogs who failed did so because the handler fell into the trap of trying to second-guess the track-layer, out-guess the dog, or compensate for what appeared to him as a situation too difficult for the dog to handle. Even the most skillful professional handler will occasionally yield to the temptation of asserting his intellectual superiority over the dog. More often than not it is the handler who defeats the dog, rather than the difficulty of the trail.

Concern is frequently expressed about certain conditions of terrain or weather which may have an adverse effect upon how the dog works or upon the trail itself. It is true that many weather conditions such as extreme heat, bitter cold, heavy precipitation or high winds make it unpleasant or uncomfortable for the dog just as they do for us. Such extreme conditions, however, need not defeat the dog. It is true that some weather conditions have an adverse effect upon a trail, making it more difficult to follow, but dogs tested in every kind of weather have clearly demonstrated that there is no such condition which will, within a reasonable length of time, obliterate or confuse the trail to the extent that the dog cannot follow it.

The same holds true with respect to conditions of terrain. Certainly hot sand, rough, frozen ground or dense undergrowth are difficult or uncomfortable for both dog and handler, but not impossible. There also are many types of ground cover unfavorable to the dog following a trail, but an airborne trail is always present and we know that the dog will rely upon it when the ground trail becomes difficult. Changes from one form of terrain to another may alter the nature of the trail somewhat, but never to the extent that the dog can be completely confused.

To understand the futility of being concerned with these questions, consider the fact that there are some conditions which make following a trail physically difficult, but which actually have a favorable effect upon the trail itself. A track laid through dense undergrowth, for instance, may be forbidding and physically difficult to follow, but the trail itself will be particularly intensified as the airborne trail is trapped close to the ground trail, making it easier for the dog to detect and follow it.

There are literally thousands of conditions and circumstances, favorable and unfavorable, which may effect the handler, the dog or the trail. There are even more thousands of combinations of such conditions and circumstances. You cannot always choose or control them and to attempt to anticipate, account for or compensate for them is to bog yourself down in hopeless confusion.

When you send in an entry for a tracking test you may make some reasonable assumptions, within the limitations set by the American Kennel Club regulations, as to general length and form of the track to which you will be assigned. You also may assume the terrain and ground cover will be reasonable. According to the season, you may have an idea of what the range of temperature might be. Other than these, you rarely can predict what sort of conditions you might encounter. If you begin to be concerned about ground covers, weather conditions, chances of distractions and contamination or any of a number of other more trivial elements such as weight, sex, age, dress or other physical conditions of the tracklayer, you only succeed in confusing yourself and destroying your confidence in yourself and your dog. Such inconsequentials have

ILL. 3

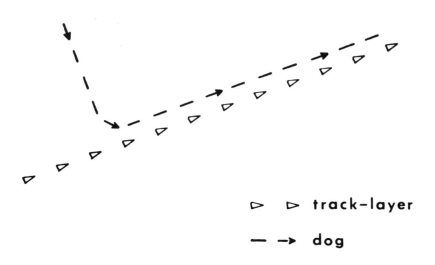

▷ ▷ **track-layer**

— —➤ **dog**

no bearing whatsoever on the quality of performance of a trained tracking dog.

Through many years of study and testing, much has been learned about dogs' consistent working behavior which can increase our understanding of and respect for the capability of the tracking dog.

It has been proven that a dog approaching a trail at right angles to it (Ill. 3) will always follow that trail in the same direction as the track-layer progressed. In addition, if the track-layer retraced his steps (Ill. 4-4A) so that there is a trail going both ways, the dog encountering it at right angles will recognize that there are two trails and that one is fresher than the other. Depending upon the type of training he has had or his own motivation, he will elect to follow one trail or the other, but he will not be confused by the presence of the double trail. If the dog is *following* a ground trail on which the track-layer has back-tracked and then turned to walk in another direction, when the dog encounters the turn he will note it and may elect to follow the trail in the direction of the turn (Ill. 5). More often, however, he will be inclined to follow the whole trail (Ill. 5A) turning to back-track where the track-layer did and make the turn off the original trail as the track-

ILL. 4

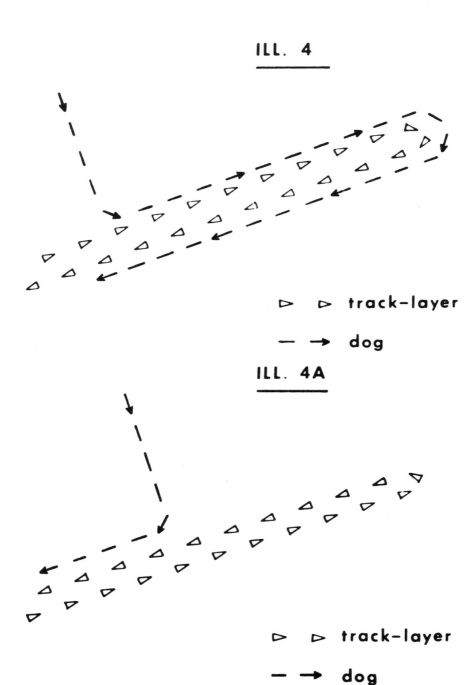

▷   ▷   track-layer

— →   dog

ILL. 4A

▷   ▷   track-layer

— →   dog

ILL. 5

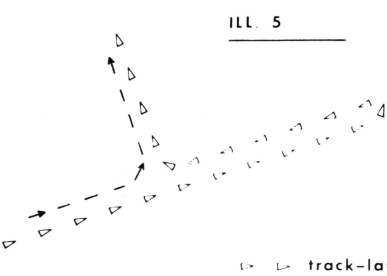

$\triangleright$ $\triangleright$ track–layer

— →   dog

ILL. 5A

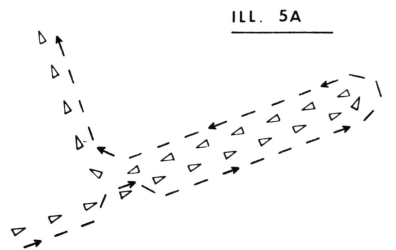

$\triangleright$ $\triangleright$ **track–layer**

— →   **dog**

layer did. If the wind in such a situation is blowing across the trail in the direction of the turn (Ill. 6) and the dog is following the airborne trail downwind of the ground trail, he usually will not follow the whole trail, but will turn to follow the fresher ground trail where he encounters it.

If the wind is blowing up from the direction of the turn and the dog is working the ground trail or the airborne trail (Ill. 6A) when he encounters the turn he will usually make the turn instead of following the whole track. This is because the presence of both the air scent and the ground trail make the trail more intense at the point of the turn in this situation.

Because the dog will follow these patterns consistently and not be confused by such seemingly complex problems, he may be trained to reverse his natural tendencies and back-track on command. This combination of consistent natural behavior and the dog's trainability is an important feature of practical tracking, particularly in search and rescue work.

A dog also is capable of detecting a "missing" person with whom he has never had any contact. In one Government experiment a group of ten people was sent into a small vacant building which they all entered by the same path and door. They remained in one room, moving about freely, for about half an hour. Then one person left by the same door and path and, a short distance away, turned from the path to lay a track across a field. Some time later a dog and handler were brought into the building. The dog was allowed to roam among the remaining nine people for a while and then commanded to go find the missing person. Although there were only nine people in the room when the dog entered, the presence of the tenth person was still there for the dog and he was able to identify that presence as physically missing and follow that trail. This was one of the most conclusive practical experiments ever made to prove the dog's ability to distinguish between individuals and demonstrate the potential usefulness of that capability.

At this point it is appropriate to comment upon the dogs used in the tests and experiments which have proven the validity of our principles of tracking. They represented a variety of breeds, mostly from the Working and Sporting groups. They were not extraordinary dogs. They were not necessarily exceptionally intelligent, but they were superior in soundness of body and temperament. If they

69

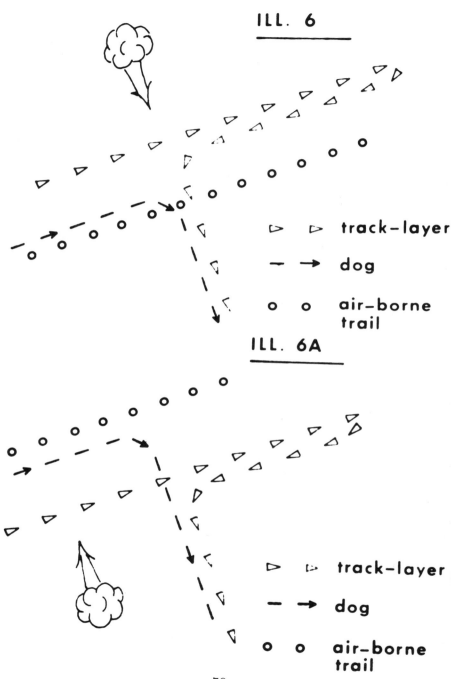

ILL. 6

track-layer

dog

air-borne
trail

ILL. 6A

track-layer

dog

air-borne
trail

70

were exceptional at all, it was by virtue of excellent training. Some were professionally trained for police and military work and some were amateur-trained pets. Surely, if such a variety of dogs, trained and handled for a wide variety of reasons, could conclusively prove these basic principles of tracking under the severe, exacting and devious methods of experimental testing, it would be apparent that any sound dog may be trained by the average person to track under everyday conditions on the basis of these same principles.

Although the following example does not apply to a trained tracking dog, it serves to illustrate the natural capability of the dog and points out the fact that those capabilities are of such a quality that while we cannot fully understand them, neither can we deny them.

Those who have run dogs in retriever trials have seen this situation occur many times. A dog and handler are in a blind near a stream. On the judge's order a gun on the opposite bank shoots a bird which drops in midstream. The dog marks the fall and another bird is shot and drops a few hundred yards from the blind (Ill. 7). The dog is directed to retrieve the second bird and does

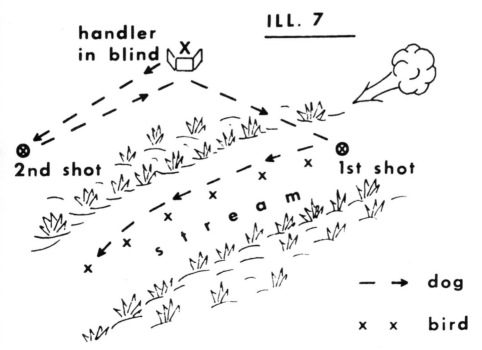

ILL. 7

handler
in blind

2nd shot

1st shot

s t r e a m

— → dog

x x bird

71

so. In the meantime, the first bird has drifted downstream with the wind behind it. When the dog is directed to retrieve the first bird, having marked the fall, he dashes into the water in that direction and, without hesitation, turns in midstream to swim after the first bird.

There is no logical explanation in human terms for how the dog knows how to handle this situation. The wind direction is wrong for him to pick up an air scent, the current is such that any scent on the water surface must have travelled downstream with the bird, and yet the dog has that dependable instinct which enables him to perform this feat time after time.

One might argue that this capability has been developed through the dog's experience and training so that he responds automatically to this situation when confronted by it. We know, however, that retrievers seldom need training to perform this feat—they *know* instinctively how to handle the situation and only need to be trained to work on command.

Research may one day give us the answers to many of our continuing questions, but we cannot presently fathom exactly what a trail is to a dog or exactly how he distinguishes and follows it. These factors are still locked in the mystery of his instinct and the function of his nervous system.

In approaching the project of training a dog for tracking we must first acknowledge our human limitations. No man can teach a dog to track. The dog already knows more about tracking than any man does. Neither can man fully understand exactly what a trail is to a dog or how he distinguishes or follows it. It is not enough, however, to admit our limitations and elect to depend solely upon the superior capability of the dog.

An untrained dog will follow a trail as he is prompted by his own motivation. If he is highly motivated by breeding or momentary incentive, he will pick up a trail and follow it to his own satisfaction. If he is not highly motivated, he may abandon the trail if he comes across the presence of more interesting or disturbing scents in the vicinity, or he may stop working when ground or weather conditions make following the trail difficult or uncomfortable. Such behavior is not an indication of inability on the part of the dog. It is the result of lack of motivation or incentive. Rather than accept such lack of motivation and blame "circumstances" for such arbitrary behavior, it is the task of the handler to train the dog to work on command, and to create incentive in the dog to follow a specifically designated trail. We know that the dog *can* follow a specific trail, regardless of even extreme adversity. Whether or not he *does* is a matter of training. Once you accept this simple approach to working with a dog in tracking, you need no longer be concerned with being at the mercy of the dog's will or physical "conditions" of the trail.

Success in training a dog for tracking can only be attained if there is absolute acceptance of control on the part of the dog and unqualified recognition by the handler of the dog's innate ability to track. You must learn to believe in your dog's capability and to trust it. You must learn to read your dog so that you know when he is working and when he is not. You must teach your dog the commands to work and train him to work under control. Finally, you must give the dog incentive, positive motivation to follow a specific trail on your command.

How to Start

THERE is nothing quite so impressive in obedience work as the spectacle of a well trained handler-dog tracking team at work on a trail. The dog creates an impression of drive and purpose. The handler exhibits confidence and assurance. Together they offer a picture of perfect teamwork. Because such a team is not a common sight at tracking tests, people often feel that accomplishing such results with their own dogs is out of reach. This need not be so.

Not every dog is naturally motivated by breeding to tracking work, but it is possible to create incentive in any dog of sound temperament to want to work for and please his handler.

Tracking is not like any other form of obedience training. It is not, and cannot be approached as an obedience exercise or series of exercises. The individual temperament of the dog plays an extremely important role in tracking. Every dog tracks as he is individually inclined and, although he may be trained to work under control, the way he tracks cannot be changed. As a trainer, you can only teach him to follow a trail on command. It might be necessary to drive one dog with a continual run of commands and encouragement, and it might be necessary to hold back another,

A well-trained tracking dog and a capable handler represent the ultimate in obedience teamwork. Both dog and handler know what to do and perform their joint function with efficiency. With the right approach virtually any dog can be successfully trained to be a capable tracker.

or be conservative in use of voice so as not to break into the dog's concentration. This is the sort of thing each handler must determine from study and understanding of his own dog. Honest understanding of the dog's temperament and capability, and willingness to work *with* him, are the foundation of the close team relationship of a handler and his dog in tracking.

Before starting to train your dog you will need certain equipment and a place to work.

Equipment

The Harness

IT is accepted practice to work a tracking dog in a harness. Use of the harness, as opposed to the slip-chain collar used in other obedience work, is popularly regarded as a means of indicating to the dog what type of work is expected of him. Although this is true to some extent, it is of minor importance. There are two reasons for use of a harness in tracking.

First, the harness allows the dog to work as he should with a maximum of comfort and efficiency. The dog must be trained to work in much the same way as a horse is trained to pull a wagon. He must work on a taut lead and literally pull you along with him as he works a track. The harness must be pliable and well-fitted so that the dog's driving force is evenly distributed across his chest and shoulders as he works. It is possible to work a trained tracking dog on a collar, but this is most unsatisfactory. A dog cannot work comfortably for any length of time on a taut lead with the pressure against his throat.

Second, and equally important, a harness provides the handler with the most reliable way to read the dog. Through a taut lead, the evenly distributed working force of the dog exerted against the harness strap across his chest allows you to feel exactly how he is working at all times.

The Lead

A 30-foot lead is adequate for any type of tracking and in any phase of training. Tracking leads usually are made of heavy cotton or synthetic webbing. Some people prefer nylon cord leads which are more compact, lighter in weight and somewhat easier to handle. The choice of lead is optional, depending upon what is most comfortable for the handler to use.

When you begin training you will work with a very short lead. Nevertheless, it is advisable to use the regular tracking lead very early in training in order to get accustomed to handling it. Reels designed for handling a tracking lead, to prevent it from becoming tangled are not recommended. Physical manipulation of the lead is extremely important in handling and reading the dog. Use of a reel will nullify much of the effectiveness of proper lead handling, particularly in reading the dog. As for the risk of the lead tangling, this rarely happens to the extent of making it necessary to stop working in order to free a caught or tangled lead.

Stakes and Articles

It is essential to work only on staked tracks until the dog is trained to the point of reliability, and you have learned to read him well enough to recognize by his behavior whether or not he is on the track. The dog, and *only* the dog, knows how to track. You cannot teach him to track. You can only train him to work for you on command. You can only train the dog to stay on a track when you know exactly where the trail is so that you know when to correct and praise him.

You will need two or three stakes. One will mark the beginning, one the end of the track and, at a later stage, one will mark the point at which a turn has been made. It is common practice to attach "flags" to the stakes, but so long as the stakes are readily visible to the handler and track-layer, flags are not really necessary.

The stakes themselves play absolutely no part in training the dog. They are used solely as markers of the ground trail for the benefit of the track-layer and handler.

The choice of an article to be left at the end of a track is optional. Most people use a glove or wallet because these are articles specifically suggested in the American Kennel Club regulations and are most frequently used in official tests. A handkerchief, shoe, cap, or any other article of like size, bearing the scent of the track-layer, will do as well.

Assistance

In the initial stages of training it is not necessary to work with another person. You know the dog has the natural ability to distinguish between individuals, and that he can follow a designated trail. Therefore, there need not be any concern about the dog learning to follow the trail of a stranger if his initial training is done on your trail alone. In the beginning you will only be concerned with teaching the dog to follow a ground trail on command. Once this has been accomplished, the dog will work *any* trail, stranger or not, because he understands what your command means.

If you prefer to work with someone else, select someone who shares your interest in tracking and is willing to cooperate with you in your approach to training.

The Tracking Field

PEOPLE often feel they cannot go into tracking unless they have access to acres of uncontaminated fields in which to work. In later training you will need larger areas, but in the beginning, an open grassy area about 75 yds. square is adequate. Such an area allows you to lay a 50 yd. track with 25 yds. of free space at either end of it.

It has been established that the dog will not be confused by the presence of the return trail of a track-layer retracing his steps. Therefore, you may use the same track several times in each training session. When doing this, caution must be exercised to walk exactly the same path, going and coming, as it is plotted by the stakes.

Re-use of the same track is not only a conservation of available space, it has certain advantages in training. Each time you work the track, it is intensified, making it easier for the dog to concentrate and understand your commands.

Training in areas contaminated by public use or exposed to public activity in the vicinity are considerations of minor importance and need not become problems. Although it would be unfair to the dog in early training to expect him to concentrate in the presence of excessive distraction, exposure to a reasonable amount of contamination and distraction is good at any stage of training. If you use school grounds, for instance, it is better to work on weekends than during the week when the grounds have been under heavy use. Choose to work at times when there is not a great deal of activity in the immediate vicinity. The dog eventually will have to work under conditions where contamination and interference or distraction cannot be completely controlled. If he is accustomed to such contingencies during training, he is less likely to be disturbed by them if encountered during practical work or a tracking test.

Commands and Encouragement

There is much less formality in tracking than in any other type of obedience work. In A.K.C. tests the handler is allowed to use any sort of command or verbal encouragement he chooses, and as often as he likes. Tracking handlers should take full advantage of this. Use commands that are natural and meaningful to yourself and the dog, and expressions of encouragement and praise that urge the dog on with the assurance that he is pleasing you.

Single-word commands such as "Track" are somehow inadequate in tracking. In the obedience ring a single-word command for a single act, done one time and finished, is quite appropriate. Tracking, however, is a team effort of dog and handler, requiring free-flowing communication. Single-word commands sound artificial and fall short of conveying to the dog what is really expected of him in the way of continuous performance.

Command expressions such as "Go find it!" are preferable to single-word commands. Such an expression states precisely what the handler wants the dog to do. It has meaning for the handler and is a natural expression into which he can put a variety of inflections that have meaning to the dog. With such an expression you can keep the dog working by conveying urgency, authority, excitement or reprimand if his attention to the trail wavers.

Encouraging the dog while he is working is extremely important. When he is working well and you know he is on the track, encouragement will drive him on and stimulate his desire to please. Here again, it is best to use an informal expression which will convey your pleasure and eagerness to go on. Something like "atta-boy!

that's it!'', spoken with enthusiasm and reassurance or excitement, can be most effective.

Some dogs need very little driving—they are highly motivated and take naturally to tracking. Such dogs may need only occasional words of encouragement and may even be distracted by too much. Other dogs need the extra incentive of constant encouragement to continue working. The amount of encouragement needed is something that can be determined only by observation of the dog in early training. A dog who learns the commands quickly and must be controlled in his eagerness to track, usually will require a conservative amount or kind of encouragement. A dog who is slow to learn the commands, is easily distracted or frequently disinterested usually will require constant encouragement.

A tracking dog should work hard, with eagerness and enthusiasm. Therefore, each handler must choose commands and encouragement which come naturally to him and with which he may most clearly express by tone of voice and inflection what he wants the dog to understand. Such expressions may also be chosen on the basis of what has meaning to the dog from previous experience. For instance, a dog trained to retrieve will react positively to a command such as "Go get it!" or "Hunt close" if he strays from the trail. A dog trained to Utility scent discrimination will understand "Go find it". A dog trained to police work will understand a command such as "Go find him" and encouragement such as "That's it—you've got him now!". It makes no difference *what* you say by way of commands or encouragement. The important thing is that what you say has meaning to your dog.

In considering this matter of commands and encouragement you will begin to get the feel of the real difference between tracking and other obedience work. You also will begin to appreciate the importance of honest communication in training and handling. In ring work the dog is trained to work *for* the handler. In tracking the dog and handler work *together* as a team. You train the dog to work on command, but because there are aspects of how the dog tracks that you cannot understand or control, you also must rely upon his natural capability and work with it. Working with a trained tracking dog might be described as man's intelligence working with animal instinct. Communication must be based on mutual understanding and respect. It is as important to convey

A dog working properly under restraint.

to the dog your confidence in him as it is to train him to work on command. Once you have attained this mutual understanding, you will have the spirit of team-work which is vital to working with a tracking dog.

Handling

From the beginning the dog must work under restraint. When you have accepted the facts that the dog already knows how to track and that he can recognize and follow a ground trail, you may dismiss from your mind any concern that the restraint of working on a taut lead will hamper or confuse him. Bear in mind that you are *not* teaching the dog to track. You are training him to follow a specific trail on your command and under your control. Working under restraint is an essential part of your control and must be part of training at all times.

The primary reason for working the dog on a taut lead is that it is the best way to read him. You can read a great deal visually, but through a taut lead you can *feel* more about how the dog is working than you can by sight. With a taut lead you can feel subtle changes in the dog's working attitude which cannot be determined as quickly or accurately by visual observation.

If you follow a person down the street, 30 feet behind him, and he slows his pace slightly, you might walk several yards before realizing his change of pace through visual awareness of the shortened distance between you. On the other hand, if that person is pulling you at the end of a 30 foot rope, you will recognize his change of pace immediately because, under the restraint of the rope, your own pace will change at the same moment. This is an extremely important factor in reading a tracking dog. Change of pace is one of the most significant signs of a change in his working attitude and might mean any of several things such as a turn, a distraction or waning of interest. Being alerted instantly to such a change of pace, through a taut lead, gives you as the handler the advantage of noting its cause and dealing with it properly whereas, if you do not note it immediately, the reason may never be known to you or known too late for you to take advantage of it.

If you start the first lesson working on a taut lead and continue

This illustration clearly indicates why a taut lead is essential in all tracking work. If the dog is on a slack lead there is no way he can be guided by his handler on a track. Also, with a slack lead the handler will be unable to sense changes of speed or attitude as they occur.

with that technique, the dog will more quickly learn to accept it and you will begin to learn to read and control the dog more effectively as you train him.

A taut lead affords the handler the best means of physical control in training. On a taut lead the dog may be kept in the immediate vicinity of the trail by guidance, without breaking into his working pace and attitude. On the other hand, if the lead is loose, the dog must be stopped if he gets off the track and then guided back by command or lead, thus interrupting the continuity of his working pace as well as his concentration. On a taut lead the dog's speed may be controlled and eventually worked into a smooth, even pace comfortable to both dog and handler. Training the dog to work at a uniform rate of speed is important. If the dog is trained to work at a steady pace, hesitation or acceleration becomes easier to detect and its significance more easily determined. Control of pace can only be attained by training the dog to work on a taut lead at all times.

There are other advantages to working with a taut lead. If uniform tautness is maintained it is easier for the handler to adapt to the attitude of the dog. Also, a taut lead is less likely to become a distraction to the dog than a loose one. A dog working on a loose lead may be distracted by unavoidable changes in position or tension of the lead. He may stop working altogether if the lead suddenly becomes taut for some reason. There is another, more subtle factor in working the dog under restraint. It's a little like the psychology of whetting a person's appetite for something by withholding it from him. Vocal urging combined with lead restraint often will act to increase the dog's drive and stimulate his interest and excitement.

Care must be taken not to yank on the lead at any time. Neither must you allow the lead to go slack lest the dog, in speeding up, suddenly comes up short as the lead becomes taut again. Anything other than uniform restraint, even in guiding the dog if he gets off the track, will have the effect of correction. If the lead is always taut there will be little risk of the dog mistakenly feeling that he is being corrected. You do not want the dog to stop working at any time in tracking. You correct him verbally. Physically you guide him out of his errors, urging him on with repeated commands and encouragement.

Incentive

INCENTIVE is the most important element in training a dog to be a good working tracker. Dogs who take naturally to tracking will eagerly seek out a trail from the first training session. Such dogs only need to be trained to work under control and on command. Others, who have less natural motivation may just stand and look at you as you try to get them to take note of the first track. Such dogs need to be given incentive devised by the trainer, creating in them a will to work and desire to follow a trail which is equivalent to the drive of the dog who is naturally motivated to tracking.

In your first training session you might create incentive by making an elaborate procedure of depositing the article at the end of a short track while the dog is watching. This serves the double purpose of arousing his curiosity and interest, and starting him out in the right direction, allowing you to concentrate on getting him to understand that he is to follow the ground trail leading to the article.

If you are working with another person, have him lay a track to a point where he is able to hide. The dog will see the track-layer disappear and will want to "go find" him.

Whatever means you choose to create incentive always keep the dog's interest alive with commands and encouragement. It is important to remember that creating incentive is only a tool, a means of getting the dog interested in what you want him to do. Your first concern must always be to teach the dog to follow a ground trail on command. He must not be allowed to simply go after the article or hidden friend. He must have his attention directed at the ground trail at all times so that he learns that you want him to "find it" by tracking.

The First Track

We now come to the point where you have found a suitable area for training, have a harness, lead, stakes and article, and are ready to proceed with training your dog.

First, we plan where the track will be plotted, the starting point and the end of the track. Once you have determined this, put the harness on the dog, take him to the point at which you intend to start the track and put him on a sit or down stay. It is important to put the harness on the dog *before* laying the track so that you do not risk losing his interest in whatever incentive you may create, by fussing with the harness after the track has been walked. Place the first stake in the ground in front of the dog, walk out in a straight line about 50 paces and place the second stake. The manner in which you walk the track makes no difference with respect to the intensity of the trail for the dog. People frequently scuff their feet in walking a track in the belief that this intensifies the trail. This does not make any significant difference in the trail at all. There may be one benefit in this technique. Scuffing may make it possible for you to see exactly where the track is, thereby reinforcing your certainty of its location, but this is the only advantage of foot-scuffing. Neither does the distance between steps or speed with which you walk the track make any difference in the intensity of the trail for the dog.

After placing the second stake, turn and face the dog, making sure he sees you drop the article on the ground. Exaggerate this action by waving or tossing the article in the air before dropping it, thereby creating an incentive in the dog to go to that spot. Retrace your steps directly to the starting point.

Leaving the dog on a stay at the first stake.

One way of creating incentive in training a tracking dog is by tossing the article in the dog's view that will be found at the second stake.

This is how the handler attracts the dog's attention to the ground trail.

Working on a short lead as the dog learns to follow a ground trail.

Attach the lead to the harness and hold it taut about six inches from the harness. In the first few training sessions it is advisable to use a regular six foot training lead. You will have to use your tracking lead as soon as the dog has begun to learn the commands and will work ahead of you several feet. In the first few lessons, however, it is better not to be concerned with getting accustomed to the tracking lead since you should concentrate on teaching the dog what is expected of him on your command.

It is important to remember that only the dog knows how to track. Your concern is to teach him to work on your command. Since you really only know the exact location of the ground trail, you must ignore the presence of the airborne trail, the location of which you do not know, so that you can correct the dog when he is wrong and praise him when he is right.

Attract the dog's attention to the trail by pointing to or tapping the ground with your free hand immediately in front of him, indicating to him where you know the ground trail to be. At the same time give the "go find it" command with overtones of authority, urgency or excitement.

As soon as the dog's attention is drawn to the ground and he indicates his awareness of or interest in the trail, encourage him with a meaningful phrase such as "that's it!" Repeat the command if necessary to maintain the dog's attention to the trail, and continue to point to the ground ahead of him in the direction of the second stake. As the dog moves forward, move with him, urging him on, encouraging his interest in the trail.

It is wise to work beside the dog at first so that you can keep his attention directed to the ground trail by indicating it with your hand. You must also be close enough to guide him easily as he learns the meaning of your commands. The lead must be kept short and taut to prevent the dog from straying off the track.

In the first few lessons do not expect to be able to maintain uniform lead tautness, nor expect to be able to keep the dog's attention constantly on the ground trail. Every dog works and learns differently. You will not know how your dog works until you start training him. He may tend to move from side to side, or may raise his head from time to time as if looking for something. He may pull wildly, or he may work in spurts—stopping and starting. In any case, if you maintain lead length and position, never allow yourself to get off the track, and maintain forward progress, you will find lead tension easier to control. Consistency in lead handling will enable the dog to learn more quickly. If you work on too long a lead with which you cannot smoothly control the dog, the resultant erratic control will seem inconsistent and confusing to the dog.

As soon as you have worked your way to the second stake and the dog has designated the article, praise him lavishly. Walk a few yards beyond the end of the track and let the dog play with the article for a few minutes. This will serve the double purpose of letting him know he has done what you wanted and stimulated his interest and incentive. Return to the first stake with the dog close at heel, taking care to stay precisely on the original track so that you do not leave a confusing side-trail. Repeat this procedure in its entirety three or four times and then stop before the dog gets bored, or you get impatient.

Once the dog will work a few feet ahead of you and only needs a command to direct his attention to the ground trail, it is time to begin using the tracking lead. If you arrange the lead in a series of long, flat loops, once it is snapped on the harness it may be dropped to the ground and will feed out as you move away, much as a coiled rope would.

There are several things to bear in mind as you work the first few tracks and during all early training. Remember that you must observe carefully your dog's manner of following the trail. Observe his physical attitudes—position of head, ears, tail, etc.—when you *know* he is on the trail and working. These observations will become vitally important when you begin to work unknown tracks and must rely entirely upon the dog's capability and training and your ability to read him. You should also note how he follows a trail. He may tend to cast from side to side or work straight ahead, seeming to seek out the trail several feet ahead of him. He may be a slow, deliberate worker, seeming to investigate every blade of grass along the way. Such observations of the dog's natural way of working a track are important because you must learn to adapt to them in training and handling. You cannot and must not attempt to change the dog's natural manner of tracking, but you can control it. If you have a dog with natural motivation and drive, your training will consist mostly of teaching commands and exercising control.

If you have a slow worker, you will have to concentrate on creating additional incentive and use of commands and encouragement to drive the dog along.

You will begin to learn to read the dog through the lead during your early training sessions. You will feel the way he works, the amount of pull he exerts when he is on the trail, the release of tension when he is momentarily distracted or casting. Learning to read the dog through a taut lead in early training, while still working on staked tracks, is very important. You should be proficient at reading your dog through the lead before you begin to work unknown tracks. Confidence in your ability to read your dog is essential to the success of that step in training. If you neglect the importance of learning to read the dog in early training you will find working unknown tracks more confusing and difficult than it should be.

The amount of restraint you use must be wisely handled in early training. With some dogs, particularly those who take naturally to tracking, working under restraint will present very few problems. With others it must be introduced gradually. In no case, however, should restraint amount to unyielding resistance. A dog who is willing to work must not get the feeling of being held back and therefore wrong.

As soon as the dog understands the command and starts following the trail, allow the lead to slip through your hands, slowly increasing your grip on it, gradually increasing the lead tension. This increase in tension should be smooth as well as gradual and should only be done while the dog is actually working the track. As you encourage him verbally, continue moving with the dog at a slightly slower pace than his as the lead slips through your hands. The dog will feel he is right and will begin to accept restraint. As he begins to understand what is expected of him, the degree of restraint may be gradually increased in each practice session until he fully accepts the idea that he is to pull you along as he works.

As noted earlier, unless you know the exact location of the trail you cannot properly correct the dog when he is wrong, or praise him when he is right. The dog will be aware of the airborne trail as soon as he is aware of the ground trail and may be inclined to check it from time to time. Do not allow this. Even though the dog knows where the airborne trail is, you do not. Therefore, you cannot control his working of the airborne trail. Until you have learned to read the dog accurately, you cannot even be certain if inattention to the ground trail is prompted by an interest in the airborne trail or by something else. Once trained, you know the dog will work one trail or the other, depending upon which is easier for him under prevailing conditions, but in the beginning you should only be concerned with teaching him the command to work. You can only accomplish this under controlled conditions, restricting yourself and the dog to working a known ground trail.

If knowing where the article is or where the track-layer is hidden has created an incentive in the dog, you must make sure he is not merely "sight" working in that direction. Since you will work right beside the dog, or on a relatively short lead, the full distance of the first few tracks, it will not be difficult to make certain his attention is always directed to the ground trail. If the dog hesitates and looks searchingly ahead toward the end of the track, redirect his attention to the ground immediately by pointing on it in front of him and repeat the command to "go find it".

Be persistent in maintaining the dog's attention to the ground trail. Do not let him be distracted by sights and sounds in the vicinity. If he is easily distracted, use a harsher tone of voice in repeating the command, and more encouragement and praise when he gets back to work.

There is no place in tracking for force training. At no time should you force the dog's head down or press his nose to the ground or drag him along a track. Any such use of force nullifies whatever incentive the dog may have been given, and destroys the positive will to work which is so vital in tracking. You can force a dog to sit or lie down as part of training him to do so on command, but you cannot force a dog to track.

Even though you may have a dog who takes to tracking readily and offers no problems with respect to working under restraint, don't rush your training. As the dog begins to follow a track and stay with it, drop back five or six feet at first—far enough to allow him to get the feel of pulling you, but close enough to guide him easily if he begins to stray from the trail. As he becomes more dependable, gradually increase the lead length each time you work until he is working 10 to 20 feet ahead of you. Do not increase the distance, however, unless he is pulling you and is consistently staying with the trail, or reacts promptly to verbal commands if he gets off the trail. If he begins to show lack of concentration or control, shorten the lead again until you can be sure of his dependability.

Work only on single-leg, straight tracks until the association between the command and following the ground trail is firmly implanted in the dog's mind and he always directs his attention to the ground trail when he hears the command to "go find it". It will take only a few sessions to accomplish this with some dogs. Others will take longer and will require more patience. This is no reflection on the dog's ability to track, but only indicates a need for more incentive to supplement the lack of natural motivation, and a need for more training and control.

When you set out to train a dog for tracking you should be prepared to work and practice on a regular schedule. Three sessions a week is ideal, but you should plan to work no less than once a week. These early training periods should be fairly short, the tracks should not be long, and it is not advisable to work a dog on a track more than five or six times at one training session. The length of any training period will best be determined by the dog's interest and the handler's patience. If either of these begins to lapse, it is time to stop and wait a few days before getting back to it again.

The First Turn

The first turn should be introduced only when you are sure the dog fully understands that he is to follow the ground trail on your command. This is extremely important because when you confront the dog with his first turn you must let *him* make the decision as to which way to go.

Start the first leg exactly as before. Leave the dog on a stay near the first stake. Walk straight out to the second stake, make a right angle turn in either direction and continue another 50 paces. Never make a turn less than 90°. This will minimize the chance of the dog air-scenting the second leg before arriving at the turn. Put the third stake in the ground and drop the article. Return to the starting point by the same route, exercising the usual precautions to stay on the same path.

As soon as the dog gets to the turn stake, watch carefully for his reactions. He will slow down and possibly stop. When you see or feel the dog's first hesitation, stop moving and remain facing the same direction. Back up a few steps if necessary to keep the lead from going slack. It is important that you do not stop the dog from working simply because *you* know he has passed the turn. You must let him work it out for himself and you must stop only when you honestly feel or see a change in the dog's attitude indicating that he realizes he is no longer on the trail.

After the dog's first hesitation, and upon your repeat of the command, he should begin to actively look for the trail. He may begin to circle, sometimes raising his head as if trying to catch wind of the trail. He may cast in his search, moving from side to side in ever-widening arcs. On a short lead, 10 to 20 feet, he will not get far off the track in any direction from the turn and should soon come across it in his casting or circling.

As long as the dog is working, you must hold your ground and remain facing in the direction you were facing when you stopped. You must not guide the dog, but you should keep him working with repeated commands and encouragement. On a 10 to 15 foot lead you should be able to detect a change in the dog before you have arrived at or passed the turn yourself. If not, back up slowly until you are a good 10 feet from the turn so that the dog will have ample opportunity to recover the trail.

If the dog has difficulty and becomes confused or loses interest, back up even further, gradually working him back to a point where he is bound to pick up the trail on the first leg, and allow him to proceed toward the turn once more and try again.

As soon as you know by sight that he has recovered the trail past the point of the turn, tell him "that's it!" and urge him on with repeat of the command. Then, and *only* then, do you turn in the direction of the second leg and go with the dog.

When working a track to be used again take care not to cut across the turn yourself or allow the excess lead to drag diagonally across the turn as the dog begins to work the second leg. If this happens there will be a second trail (Ill. 8) when the dog works the track the second time. You must stay on the track as you originally walked it and either carry the excess lead or be sure to drag it around the outside of the turn stake (Ill. 8A).

100

The dog is casting at the turn in order to determine at which point the trail continues.

The dog has committed himself to a turn and the handler follows on the tracking lead.

101

The most important feature of the first turn is that the dog solves the problem alone. It is for this reason that the first turn should never be attempted until you are certain the dog understands that he is to work the trail on command. The way the dog handles his first turn will be a real test of his training and will tell you if he needs more practice or more incentive.

The main reason for letting the dog make the turn without guidance is that it will teach him that he must seek out the trail when it seems to have disappeared. He will have to do this when you are working unknown tracks, and if you guide him, even by so much as facing in the right direction, he will come to depend upon that guidance. This will cause the dog to be undependable on turns while working unknown tracks.

Allowing the dog to work out the first and all subsequent turns is also a big step for you as a handler. It will call for self-discipline to hold your ground, steadfastly refusing to give the dog any guidance. If you are honest and strict with yourself in this, it will serve you well when you begin to work unknown tracks. First, you will have learned to rely upon the dog and you will have confidence in his ability and training. Confidence is a prime ingredient of good tracking. Second, having schooled yourself this way, you will be less likely to try to second-guess the track-layer on an unknown track and thereby run the risk of misguiding the dog.

The first few turns may be tedious. You will have to be very patient. It may be necessary to back up several times before the dog finally solves the problem. Once the dog has the idea, it will be well worth the time, patience and self-control, when you realize that you *know* you can rely upon your dog to work out a turn.

There are aspects of early training which must be emphasized.

Patience on the part of the handler-trainer is vital. You are trying to develop in the tracking dog a positive will to work. Although you may insist through repetition of commands and tone of voice, do not resort to discipline, force or sharp physical correction. This brings us back to the importance of having laid the groundwork of discipline and control through basic training. The dog who already understands and accepts control will respond to the modified control exercised in training him for tracking.

The importance of training only on staked or otherwise known tracks must also be emphasized. Once the dog has successfully

ILL. 8

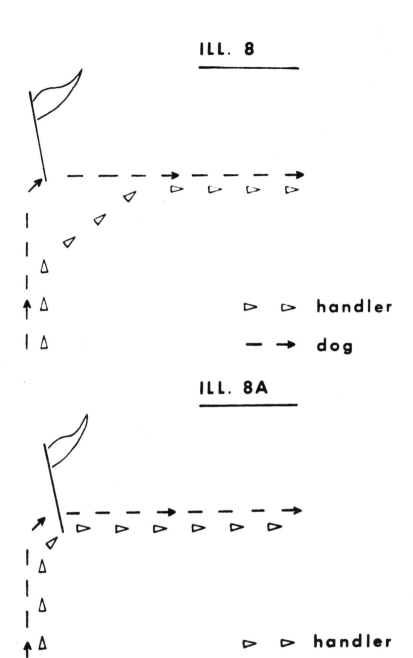

⊳ ⊳ handler

— → dog

ILL. 8A

⊳ ⊳ handler

— → dog

worked a staked track you may be tempted to have a friend lay an unstaked track for you just to see how the dog will do it. This defeats the purpose of training. You already know that the dog can and will, for whatever reason of his own, follow a trail. Remember that you are training the dog to work under your direction and you cannot achieve this if you allow him to track arbitrarily during early training. He may or may not perform successfully if you experiment prematurely with unknown tracks. You will never be sure, however, if the dog's performance in such an ill-timed experiment was the result of training or pure chance. Failure in such an experiment constitutes a set-back in training. The dog will not have learned anything and may become confused. Failure also will undermine the confidence you must have in the capability of your dog.

Concern frequently is expressed about the dog becoming "stake-wise" in early training. This is to say that the dog learns to work by sight from stake to stake. If proper attention is given to directing the dog's attention to the ground trail at all times, this should not be a problem. Any interest the dog may show in a stake he comes upon is perfectly natural since it will have been handled by the track-layer and will also have collected some of the airborne trail. In such an instance, the dog's attention may be redirected to the ground trail by command without any real interference with his training.

If you wish to use land-marks instead of stakes, caution must be exercised in choosing such land-marks. They must be easily recognized and in the immediate training area. A tall bush or tree, for example, may be used instead of a stake. Distant land-marks should never be used since they do not adequately pinpoint the location of the trail.

The means you use to create incentive in the dog should be simple and natural, and used *only* to stimulate his interest and will to work. Overdoing the creation of incentive can actually distract the dog from the main purpose of your training.

There are no short-cuts in training a dog for tracking. You must work patiently, step by step, making certain that each step in training is thoroughly understood by the dog before proceeding to the next step. Don't try to speed things up by such devices as using a "baited" track. This is a technique reserved for the dog who presents a real problem with respect to incentive, and should never be used if it is not necessary.

Never let yourself begin making excuses for the dog because of the weather, ground cover, shoes of the track-layer or anything other than the need for more incentive. Start to train in the season of the year when there will be no extremes of weather to contend with. Find three or four locations which offer a reasonable variety of ground conditions and environment. See that you or your track-layer wear different clothes and use a variety of articles. You will soon prove to yourself how unimportant these things are. At the same time you will accustom the dog to variety which will lessen the risk of his becoming dependent upon one set of conditions.

In conclusion, keep in mind the three basic principles of tracking, and never neglect the importance of communication and control. As a handler, you must believe in the dog's innate ability to follow a trail. As a trainer, you must have instilled in the dog a willingness to work and a desire to please. With this foundation, plus patience and persistence, training a dog for tracking can and should be an exciting and rewarding experience for both you and your dog.

Tracking Problems

THE previous chapter outlines the basic procedure in beginning to train a dog for tracking. It is fully recognized, of course, that no system of training will produce uniform results with all dogs. Dogs are individuals and respond differently to training. Some are more adaptable by breed than others. Most of the Working, Sporting and Hound breeds will adapt more readily to tracking than most Toy breeds. Even within the groups we find some breeds more adaptable than others. Regardless of breed, individual temperament plays a large part in determining the amount of work necessary to train a dog for tracking.

It is at the level of individual temperament that we encounter the problem dog. Since a dog is rarely purchased specifically for his tracking ability, one must be prepared for the possibility of having to cope with a dog who does not take readily to tracking and is therefore more difficult to train. Regardless of the nature or degree of the problem, its solution must be approached from the standpoint of devising additional incentives.

The most common problem is getting the dog to work ahead of the handler and pull as he follows the trail. Not only is this a common problem, but insufficient attention to overcoming it is the root of many subsequent problems which must be attributed to the dog not having been given adequate incentive in early training. Incentive should be a primary concern in the dog's first training sessions. Incentive problems may be manifested in a number of ways—apathy, lack of concentration, reluctance to "go out" from the handler, refusal to work under restraint.

Reluctance to move out ahead of the handler is a problem frequently encountered with dogs who have been obedience trained to work closely at heel whenever on lead. To overcome this, a situation must be created which will cause the dog to *want* to pull away from the handler. One way of accomplishing this is to turn the dog over to another person, preferably one who understands how to handle the dog, so that the owner may walk the track to a point where he is able to hide. The dog will want to get back to his owner and will have observed where he has gone out of sight. Finding his owner will become the main concern of the dog and he will usually pay little heed to the idea of remaining at heel with the other person. The substitute handler will give the command to "go find" and direct the dog's attention to the ground trail left by the owner. Praise and encouragement as soon as the dog moves forward are most important, as is insistence upon his maintaining attention to the ground trail. Using the same track several times becomes an advantage in this situation. After the first use of the track, the dog will be aware of both the owner's and the other person's trail. When the owner has walked the track a few times, the other person should walk the same track and hide. The incentive to follow his owner's trail will remain with the dog as he follows the trail of the other person when his owner resumes handling. This technique may also be applied to the dog whose interest is hard to arouse and maintain.

Another method of overcoming lack of interest is to capitalize on the dog's natural love of the chase. While the handler holds the dog at the first stake, another person should walk the track. About half-way out, the track-layer will turn and call the dog and then turn back to run the remaining distance to a point where he is able to go out of sight. Once the track-layer is out of sight, the handler will give the command to "go find", making certain to keep the dog's attention directed to the ground trail as he pursues the track-layer to his hiding place. Once the dog's interest in chasing the track-layer is stimulated he should be encouraged by the handler with inflections of excitement to keep his interest from flagging. This method of stimulating interest can be most effective if you are able to work near a woods. In this case, the track-layer may enter the woods and proceed a short distance beyond the point of entry, causing the dog to continue to seek him out by scent beyond the point of his disappearance.

The problem of the obedience trained dog who is reluctant to pull in harness is found particularly in one who has had to be corrected for forging in earlier obedience training. The running track-layer may help to overcome this problem, but if it persists, additional incentive may be created in play. With the dog in harness and on lead, roll a heavy, solid ball such as a croquet ball along the ground and encourage the dog to chase it. Since you are merely attempting to get the dog accustomed to the idea of pulling, don't concern him with trailing the ball. Encourage him to chase it by sight, increasing resistance on the lead gradually until he is actually pulling you along with him. Again, praise and encouragement are of supreme importance as the dog accepts more lead resistance and his interest in chasing the ball overcomes his reluctance to accept working on a taut lead. Once the dog readily pulls you in pursuit of the ball, with no sign of hesistation due to restraint, it is time to proceed with training. During such play procedure, use of the same phrases of command and encouragement to be used in later tracking work will ease the transition from the game to the first phases of training.

With certain dogs, using the food-reinforcement method (the "baited" track) will create additional incentive effectively. However, the baited track should be used as a means of creating additional incentive *only* as a last resort, when all other methods have failed. This is solely a means of creating a desire to "go out" in pursuit of something to eat. In order for it to work effectively the dog must be quite hungry. It is for this reason that the food-reinforcement method is recommended only as a last resort. Tracking should be regarded as a sport to be enjoyed by both dog and handler. Depriving the dog of normal feeding in order to make this method work can take the enjoyment out of the training process. Using this method casually as a short-cut can be disastrous and actually create additional training problems which might have been avoided by using the natural methods with a dog who is not really that difficult to train for tracking.

If you feel you must resort to food-reinforcement, deprive the dog of one day's feeding. As you walk the track, place several small amounts of food at varying distances along the trail. Make sure the dog knows you have food and let him see you drop it as you walk the track. Use the same commands and encouragement you would normally use and make sure to direct the dog's attention to the ground trail as you work with him. Each time you work a track, vary the distances between the pieces of food. Gradually reduce the number of pieces until there is only one at the end of the track with the article. By the time you get to this point the dog should have gotten the idea of tracking and your incentive problem should be solved. With sufficient emphasis on praise and encouragement the food may be eliminated and praise should be sufficient reward. As you reduce the number of food particles you should also gradually reduce the degree of the dog's hunger to the point where the dog has been fed normally when you arrive at the stage of eliminating the bait.

There are other food-reinforcement methods of training which are not recommended under any circumstances. There is the "dragged" track where a piece of meat is dragged on a string as the track-layer walks the track. There is also the method of rubbing meat on the soles of the track-layer's shoes. These are methods occasionally used by professional trainers. Used by the amateur training a dog to enter A.K.C. tracking tests, these methods can create more problems than they solve. A dog trained on a "dragged" track will only track in pursuit of food and when he enters a tracking test where there is no bait, he will revert to whatever original problem of incentive he had in the first place. Even the enlightened tracking handler who arbitrarily uses the dragged track method will find that he has more of a problem weaning the dog away from the incentive to track for food reward than if he used another method in the first place. The object of tracking as a sport, or even tracking for practical or professional reasons, is to train the dog to follow a human track. For this reason, any use of food-reinforcement must be regarded as creating an additional training problem. The dog must still be trained to track a human. Stick

110

to the use of the human trail in training your dog as much as possible.

In training and practice, turns frequently present difficulties for dogs who appear to work well otherwise. This problem often persists throughout training and carries over into tracking tests where most failures occur at turns. For this reason, turns are often regarded as a problem. It is not uncommon to hear people claim that their *only* problem is turns. These people usually practice on tracks which have many turns and frequently make the mistake of guiding the dog or showing him where a turn has been made. Far from helping the dog or enhancing his training, this weakens his reliability and teaches him nothing.

If you think you have a problem with turns, ask yourself a few questions. Does the dog really have a positive will to work even though he completes single-leg tracks successfully? Does he do it with no real interest or enthusiasm? If your honest appraisal of your dog's work produces a negative answer, your problem is lack of incentive. You must go back to single-leg tracks and create additional incentive, a greater will in the dog to not merely follow a trail but actively seek it. Also ask yourself if the dog has a thorough understanding of your commands and positive reaction to your praise and encouragement, or if he just follows a trail because it is there and he knows more from exposure and practice what's expected of him than from real understanding of commands and praise. If the dog does not respond instantly to a single command or verbal communication, he has not had enough practice or you have not devoted sufficient attention to teaching him the commands. Until the dog *does* understand and reacts instantly to your commands he is not ready to meet the challenge of working out turns.

Inadequate incentive or will to work or insufficient practice and understanding of commands are the *real* problems of the dog who has persistent difficulty with turns. It is never too late to go back to single-leg tracks to reinforce the foundation of the dog's training. That foundation is too important to neglect.

Let us now move from the problem dog to the problem handler. Handler errors far out-number dog errors, particularly with respect to training.

One mistake handlers frequently make is to neglect the impor-

111

tance of working the dog under restraint. There is, in fact, a school of thought which recommends allowing the dog to work on a loose lead. This is justified on the basis of the fact that the dog has the natural ability to track and once the trail is indicated to him, he will follow it with no control necessary other than verbal commands and encouragement. The fallacy in this approach lies in the confusion which is liable to arise in the mind of the free-tracking dog between his natural instinct to track and his desire to please his handler. The dog may start out on the track, knowing he is right because his handler praises and follows him. The word "follow" is the key to the beginning of the confusion of purpose in the dog's mind. As long as the handler merely follows, the dog will go. If the handler stops, the dog will stop. If the handler turns in another, direction, the dog will turn in that direction, whether the trail goes that way or not. If the dog comes upon the more interesting trail of a wild animal and turns to follow it, so long as the handler follows him, he will think he is right. Unless the dog is trained and worked under restraint the handler is deprived of the surest way of knowing whether or not the dog is still working, and the dog is deprived of the constant reminder he needs to stay on the job. A dog allowed to work free of physical control can hardly be said to have been trained at all.

The most serious problem resulting from allowing the dog to work free of lead restraint occurs at turns, particularly in the case of a fast-working dog. Regardless of working speed or type of handling, most dogs will over-shoot a turn, even if it is only by a foot or so, simply on momentum. A fast-moving dog frequently will over-shoot by several yards. The dog's awareness of the absence of the trail will first manifest itself in a hesitation but he will tend to continue to seek out the trail ahead of him at first, carrying him even further past the turn. On a loose lead, this might also carry the handler past the turn before he realizes through visual observation that the dog is no longer on the trail. In such a situation, the handler is liable to be confused as the dog casts over a wide area, even behind the handler, and is still unable to pick up the continuation of the track. On a taut lead, the handler is immediately aware of the first hesitation of the dog and able to increase the restraint on the lead and slow his own pace so that the dog

112

remains within the immediate area of the turn. This increases his chances of picking up the trail again with a minimum of casting. The factor of the dog feeling that he is pleasing his handler also plays a large part in "turn failures" on a loose lead. Even though the dog is aware of having lost the trail, the fact that his handler is still following him will make him tend to go straight ahead in the belief that this is what his handler wants.

Any discussion of restraint brings us to the subject of reading the dog. There is no set way of reading a dog which will apply to all of them. People who have trained several dogs in tracking know that they must still learn to read each individual dog as they begin to work with him.

People frequently don't realize that they have a problem with respect to reading their dogs, or don't appreciate the importance of it, until they begin to work unknown tracks. Suddenly they feel helpless and realize that they don't really know what the dog is doing, whether or not he is actually working a trail. Many people don't even think about learning to read the dog until they get to this stage of training. This attitude reduces reading of the dog to mere guess-work.

Once they understand the commands and have developed a will to work, most dogs will work a trail with individual consistency. Reading the dog is not so much a matter of interpretation as of correlating certain facts and observations. If, for instance, you notice that every time the dog begins to stray from a staked track, his head comes up, you have learned something about reading your dog. You will know to watch for this characteristic behavior when working unknown tracks so that you will know exactly when a repeated command is necessary. If, through a taut lead, you notice that when the dog begins to stray from the staked track his pace slows slightly or becomes uneven, you will have learned a lesson in reading your dog which will serve you well in working unknown tracks.

Don't try to out-guess the dog or over-interpret him. Stick to what you can see and feel. Correlate these facts and observations honestly and objectively. Start learning to read your dog as soon as he begins to work with some degree of consistency. Read him constantly, never let your attention wander from what he is doing.

Learning to read the dog when he is working well is just as important as learning to read him when he makes a mistake. This will play a large part in building your confidence in yourself and your dog when you work unknown tracks because you will know when he is working and when he is not.

There is another problem encountered in tracking which calls for careful attention to reading the dog. He will occasionally become aware of another leg of the track or the article as he works down-wind of one or the other. He may also become aware of some distracting scent upwind. The dog's behavior in such a situation is called "winding". If he has been trained to stay on the trail he will do so despite awareness of another portion of the track or distraction upwind. He will, however, indicate his awareness by winding. This must not be confused with his way of working the trail. When the dog is winding he will momentarily stop working. He will hesitate or stop altogether, his head will come up from the angle at which it is normally carried and he will point and appear to sniff in the direction of the distant scent. At this point the unalerted or inexperienced handler might believe that the dog has come to a turn and go with him as he seeks what has caught his attention upwind (Ill. 9). This mistake may be avoided by careful observation of how the dog works at a turn on staked tracks. Many people allow their dogs to wind, cutting turns and going off to investigate distractions, but this is not good training and only encourages the dog to work more and more arbitrarily.

Such are the major problems encountered in training a dog for tracking. It is safe to state that virtually every problem may be overcome through creation of additional incentive, thorough step-by-step training on a taut lead, proper use of commands, encouragement and praise, and meticulous attention to learning to read the dog both visually and through the lead.

There are other "problems", of course: "My dog won't work in such-and-such ground cover. My dog can't track on a windy day. My dog won't work if the track-layer was a man. My dog won't work if the track-layer wore sneakers". These are just a few typical "problems", but they are *not tracking* problems. They are superficial problems created in the mind of the handler and might more accurately be called rationalizations or excuses. If you begin to feel that you have some such problem, go back to incentive and early

ILL. 9

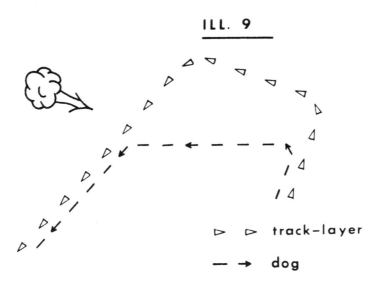

▷ ▷ track-layer

— → dog

Here the dog is starting to lift his head in the process of winding, or working from the airborne trail.

115

training. That is where your *real* problem is and that is where you will find its solution.

For the dog following a trail, tracking is an uncomplicated, natural thing to do. Therefore, you should keep your training as simple and uncluttered with invented problems as possible. Concentrate your attention on training the dog to work for you, to follow a designated trail on your command, and let the *dog* do the tracking. If he has been properly trained he can and will cope with all the minor variations of trail conditions which need be of no concern to you.

Though it is relatively unimportant, people sometimes make a "problem" of the age of a track. Many dogs are capable of following a trail which is as much as 36 hours old. Most are able to follow a trail which is 24 hours old. The American Kennel Club Regulations require that a track in an official test be at least half an hour old and no more than two hours old. This is a practical regulation made in the interests of assuring relative uniformity of conditions for all entries. It has nothing to do with the dog's capabilities.

If it will ease your mind on this matter, once the dog is working consistently well, you may start working progressively older tracks. Start with a 15 minute old track and work up to half an hour, an hour, then two hours or more. If the dog is dependable when you begin such an experiment, you will notice very little difference in his performance which would be attributable to the age of the track.

We have pointed out how and why limitation of space need not be a problem in early training by using the same track several times. This method is not only practical, it is recommended for beginners. Although you will eventually want to work in a greater variety of locations and subject the dog to more distractions, your first concern is training the dog to work on command and concentrate on the ground trail. Working in the same few locations and on re-used tracks, the dog will soon lose his curiosity about the immediate environment and minor local distractions, and his attention may be more easily maintained to the immediate matter of training. Care must be taken, of course, not to foul a track by allowing yourself to stray from it at any time. If this does happen, that track must be abandoned for a few days and another site used.

One of the most important applications of tracking training is the recovery of lost persons. This photograph was taken in an actual situation. A child had wandered into the woods and was lost. The search party and the child's mother are gathered at the point where the missing child was last seen. The mother is giving the dog the child's scent in hopes that the dog will be able to follow the trail to a successful conclusion.

Another superficial problem that often arises is finding people to act as track-layers who are strangers to the dog. Except for easing your own mind on the matter, this should be of little concern. It is possible to train a dog, with occasional assistance from one other person, to the point of being able to pass a tracking test, if the dog is trained properly. At a Government installation where six dogs were being trained for special tracking work, there were only two men assigned to train and care for the dogs. Each dog was handled consistently by the same man and worked at least three tracks a week which were laid exclusively by the other handler. Even though none of these dogs were worked on a stranger's track until after they were trained, all of them were used successfully in their very first exposure to practical tracking situations involving a stranger. Test your own dog on a stranger's track to convince yourself, but don't let it become a major concern in your training program.

Self-confidence and confidence in the dog have been mentioned several times. This is a problem which stands alone. The high incidence of lack of confidence among tracking handlers is undoubtedly due to the fact that we are working with certain unknowns. We cannot understand exactly how the dog tracks and therefore cannot completely control it. At a tracking test or in practical tracking we do not know exactly where the trail is and must rely upon the dog and his training.

Confidence must be developed through working with as many known factors as possible in early training. Therefore, you must work known tracks, learn to read the dog through careful visual observation of his natural behavior, and studious attention to the feel of his way of working as transmitted through a taut lead. When you have learned to read the dog well enough that you can anticipate his behavior in known situations, then you are ready to work unknown tracks and approach them with the knowledge that you will understand what your dog is doing even though you don't know where the trail is.

Confidence is an essential factor in handling a tracking dog. In the final analysis your confidence is two-fold and quite simple. You must first believe absolutely in the natural ability of the dog to track, and you must believe that through training he will work for you to attain successful results. The quickest way to undermine your confidence in your dog and yourself is to look for or create problems which do not exist. Work with your dog and accept the fact of his infallible instinct. Train your dog to work with you so that he knows what you expect and wants to do it. Follow these simple rules of early training and you will find that there are few real problems in tracking.

Getting Ready for
a Tracking Test

As your dog becomes more reliable, begin to work on a longer lead, lay longer tracks and include more turns. The longer the legs and the more complex the tracks, the more difficult it will become to re-use a track without fouling it. Therefore, you will need larger areas in which to work. Agricultural schools and farms, out-of-town industrial plants, areas around radio station master antenna locations, cleared land along major power lines all offer likely possibilities for longer and more varied tracks.

As you train and practice, increase the lead length gradually as the dog becomes more reliable until you are working on a 20 foot lead. Since the American Kennel Club Regulations allow you to work on a minimum 20 foot lead, there is little value in working on a longer lead while still training. The shorter the lead, the easier it will be to read the dog and control him when necessary. In addition, the dog will respond more readily, and usually will work better on a 20 foot lead than on a 40 foot lead—the maximum length allowed in the Regulations.

The length of your tracks and number of turns also may gradually be increased as the dog becomes more proficient and your confidence increases. Vary the length of the legs from 50 to 150 yards, and vary the angles of the turns between very slight turns and right angle turns. Never make the turns less than 90°. If you make an acute angle turn, you create a situation in which the dog may pick up the scent of the next leg before he gets to the turn, especially if it is downwind (Ill. 10-10A). This may confuse you as the handler, since the dog may be tempted to cut the corner instead of following the whole track.

Continue the practice of staking your tracks unless you have land-marks which will pinpoint each turn beyond any possibility of error or confusion.

How often or how long you work will depend largely upon the dog. You should work at least once a week, but do not overdo it. Some dogs can work every day and still enjoy tracking. Others get bored if they are required to work more than once or twice a week or more than one track at each practice session. Since the dog's enthusiasm is a vital factor in his working attitude and ultimate success, you must adapt your training schedule to his capacity for enjoyment of tracking.

As you progress and the dog successfully completes many tracks with long legs and several turns, you should begin to work unstaked, unknown tracks. This will require the assistance of another person to act as track-layer. Always try to work with someone familiar with or interested in tracking who either understands what is required of a track-layer or is willing to follow your specific instructions.

The track-layer should make a chart as he walks the track, noting landmarks which will pinpoint the direction of each leg of the track and the turns. It also is a good idea if he counts his paces so that he has an approximate idea of the length of each leg of the track. If the dog has been properly trained it will not confuse him to have the track-layer follow at a distance of about 30 feet as you work the track in order to alert you promptly if you or the dog make an error from which it might be difficult to recover. This is not to say that the track-layer will actually guide you as you work. He should not, for instance, tell you the dog has arrived at a turn unless it is obvious that you have not been able to deter-

ILL. 10

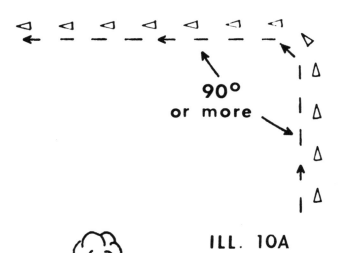

**90°
or more**

ILL. 10A

less than 90°

▷   ▷   track–layer

━ ➔   aog

mine that fact through reading the dog, and are allowing him to get too far away from the track, or if you are about to pass the turn yourself. Even when the track-layer must alert you, he should merely do so with a comment such as "hold your ground" or "back up" rather than, "There's a right turn at that clump of goldenrod". On the other hand, the track-layer should also let you know when you are holding the dog back from doing the right thing. In such cases he should not tell you which way the track goes, but simply tell you to "go with the dog".

The main thing you want to accomplish in working unknown tracks is the development of your confidence in the dog and confidence in your handling and reading of the dog. Guidance from the track-layer should therefore be minimal and only directed at pointing out your mistakes or those of the dog rather than telling you where the track is. In working unknown tracks you should concentrate on allowing the dog to work out the track on his own as much as possible. At the same time you should begin to rely upon what you have learned about reading the dog.

As you begin to work unknown tracks, remember that you are still training. You will correct the dog as required, but since you cannot correct unless you know where the trail is, it is important to have the track-layer immediately available so you know when and for what to correct. Although you should not use firm lead correction in early training, once you are sure the dog knows what is expected of him, you may begin to make lead corrections and harsh verbal corrections when the dog yields to a distraction or his attention wanders despite your commands. You must be certain, however, that the dog is wrong when making such corrections. If you correct the dog erroneously when he knows he is right, it will confuse him and lessen his willingness to work. Willingness to work is so essential in tracking that you must take every precaution to preserve it, especially if you have had to overcome problems of incentive in early training.

The choice of a track-layer must be made carefully. When you begin to work unknown tracks you will be testing yourself even more than the dog. When a mistake is made and you go off the track it is as liable to be your mistake as it is the dog's. The person working with you must be capable of judging this accurately so as to let you know what the mistake is and at the right moment for you to see and rectify it.

Once you begin to work unknown tracks, do not neglect the importance of also working staked tracks frequently. This will serve to sharpen your ability to read the dog and will continue to improve the dog's confidence and working ability since you will be able to correct and praise effectively.

When you begin to work unknown tracks it is important to bear in mind that the dog can work either the ground trail or the airborne trail or both, depending upon favorability of conditions to him. The dog should be working 20 to 30 feet ahead of you, allowing him freedom to choose which trail to work. Since, on an unknown track, you will not know where the ground trail is, you cannot be sure which trail he is working. You must rely upon what you have learned about reading the dog to tell you he is working as trained.

Unless you understand the nature of the airborne trail, it might seem that the dog is working erratically on what you know to be a straight-line ground trail. The use of the word "air" in this term confuses many people. The airborne trail is not actually in the air. It is deposited *through* the air onto dense objects or surfaces downwind of the ground trail by the air passing over the body of the track-layer as he moves. On a still day it may drift only a few feet. On a windy day it may be carried several yards. In areas of uneven ground cover or terrain it will be deposited in varying degrees of intensity, and on flat, even terrain with a certain degree of uniformity. This is not to say that a certain amount of "scent" is not in the air, particularly on a still, sunny day when radiation causes the scent to rise and linger in the air over the ground trail. This is *not,* however, the airborne trail and the dog will not follow it since the presence of the stronger ground trail and air*borne* trail are easier for him to follow. The only time a dog follows an air scent is when he is "winding". When allowed to, he works toward whatever he is winding until he comes upon the actual trail whence he will follow it, whether it be a ground trail or airborne trail. (Ref. Ill. 9 on "winding".)

As you work unknown tracks, note the wind direction and how it relates to each leg as you work. This will help you to understand the dog's behavior and give you a clue as to the probable area of the ground trail. The airborne trail will be deposited on high objects which may range in size from a thick fir tree to a single clump of grass only a few inches higher than the surrounding ground cover. It will be deposited in low spots which may be as shallow as a depression left by the removal of a stone or as large as a drainage ditch or gully. If you have noted the wind direction it will be obvious that the dog seems to be checking downwind of the general direction in which he is working. As long as you are sure he is working, this should not be corrected on unknown tracks. Repeating the command to "go find" will keep his attention on working the track whether he is working the ground trail or the airborne trail.

You may deliberately set up a few tracks in order to observe just how the dog will work an airborne trail. Lay a track parallel to and about 10 feet from a hedgerow at a time when the wind will blow across your trail toward the hedgerow. You may also lay a track diagonally across a furrowed field when the wind is blowing across the field in a direction perpendicular to the furrows. In the first case you will observe the dog check the hedgerow frequently or actually work the full distance along side of it with his attention centered on the hedgerow itself. In the second case (Ill. 11) you will note that the dog will tend to work a zig-zag pattern, checking down the furrows where the airborne trail has settled as he works in the general direction of the ground trail.

Even though you feel sure the dog is well trained, do not neglect the importance of driving him on with repeat of commands and encouragement. You and the dog should be a working team. The dog needs constant reminding of this through verbal communication, uniform lead restraint and working at a uniform pace.

The pace at which the dog works is largely determined by his individual temperament and incentive. Highly motivated dogs who take quickly and eagerly to tracking often must be slowed down. A fast working dog is impressive to watch but there are certain disadvantages to working with such a dog. Fast workers often overshoot turns to the extent that a great deal of casting is required to recover the track. Also, the faster the dog is allowed to work, the more difficult it becomes to read him. Then there is the matter of human endurance. Unless the handler is able to keep pace with

ILL. 11

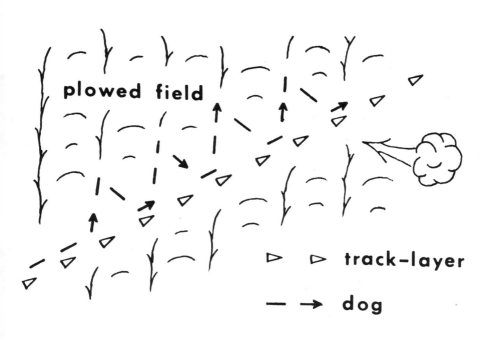

plowed field

▷   ▷   track-layer

— →   dog

the dog, without losing his footing or becoming winded, he is liable to find himself in trouble. If the handler must slow down on his own account, the dog, unable to understand why he is being held back, is liable to feel he is wrong or have his attention diverted by the change of attitude and pace of the handler. Regardless of the speed at which the dog may be able to work, it is recommended that no dog be allowed to work at a pace which requires more than a walking attitude from the handler.

Fast or slow, the pace must be determined by the rate at which the dog works most comfortably under restraint. Uniformity of pace also is important. Once the dog understands what is required of him and works consistently under restraint, you will find that he sets his own pace. Changes of pace by the handler make it difficult to maintain uniform tension on the lead. This in turn makes it difficult to read the dog and tends to distract him as he works.

When you first start to work unknown tracks, turns become particularly important. Each turn is a true test of the dog's training and of the handler's ability to read the dog and trust him. At this stage of training, be honest with yourself. Do not yield to the temptation to out-guess the track-layer or the dog.

Your first indication of a turn will come through a slackening of lead tension as the dog becomes aware of having lost the trail. Visually you will note that he begins to cast in a random manner from side to side or in a circular fashion. He may lift his head as if trying to pick up the trail by winding. At this point do not attempt to follow the dog as he casts. Remain facing exactly the same direction as when you first felt the slackening of the lead. Do not allow the dog to wander over a wide area. To maintain lead tension as the dog casts, back up slowly, gradually working the dog back to where you are sure he can once again pick up the trail at a point before he hesitated. All the while, keep him working with repetition of the command to "go find".

It is at such a point that lead tension will play an important part in telling you when the dog has finally committed himself to the continuation of the trail at the point of a turn. He will continue to cast with very little resistance to lead restraint, working within the area restricted by the length of·the lead. But once the dog has regained the trail, he will actually pull you. After careful observation and practice on turns, you will come to recognize that firm tug on the lead as your assurance that the dog is back on the trail.

Here again we must emphasize the importance of working with a track-layer who understands what it is you are trying to accomplish. Until you have learned to rely completely upon the dog and your reading of him, you will have to rely upon the intelligent observation of your track-layer to tell you, not necessarily when you are right, but when you are wrong. A good rule of thumb would be to let the *dog* tell you when you are right, and only let the track-layer tell you when you are wrong. This is the condition under which you will work at a test and practicing that way is excellent preparation for that event.

If you find that your confidence is not growing as it should, even though you and your dog may be completing many successful tracks, you should try injecting a few additional challenges to further test your dog and reinforce your confidence in him. Deliberately lay tracks that are more difficult than any you might expect in a test. Alternate very long legs with very short ones. Work in the rain and on windy days and at various times of day. Lay tracks through rough terrain or in areas where you will cross from one type of terrain to another. Work a track at night when you must rely completely upon the dog and your own ability to read him through the lead. Try to confuse the dog, deliberately facing the wrong direction as he casts at a turn. In any such contrived situations, a properly trained dog will eventually convince you that the combination of his natural instinct and your training has produced a good tracking dog. It should be pointed out that this sort of experimentation must not be undertaken until you are sure the dog has been thoroughly trained. This type of practice is recommended only to establish in your own mind the extent to which you may rely upon the instinct of the dog and his training.

It is also helpful to work a few tracks with another well-trained, experienced tracking dog. This will give you an objective experience in reading a dog. The subtle differences you will note between the feel of another dog and your own will point up the individual characteristics of your own dog's working patterns and attitudes.

It also will enhance your understanding and appreciation of the dog's natural capabilities if you are able to observe a field or retriever trial. Even though you may not be training a Hound or

Sporting dog, you will be able to observe the work of dogs highly motivated by breeding for scenting and retrieving. To some degree these instincts are part of every canine character. As a spectator at such a trial you may be able to spot a pattern of behavior which parallels that of your own dog. Your observations of field dogs working out their problems will help you understand better how your own dog works out the problems offered in tracking.

As you work unknown tracks you may be tempted to look for some indication of the trail other than what you can tell from reading your dog. There are many pitfalls in this. Not only do you undermine your confidence, you also increase the chance of error. There may be times when you will be able to see a trail, as on a dewy or frosty morning, and you will feel that you are enjoying an added advantage. This is possible, but don't rely on visual signs. Visual trailing is an art in itself and as a trained skill it is of great value in military scout, and search and rescue work. Unless you have been trained to be proficient in this skill do not attempt to rely on it. One not trained in visual trailing cannot know for certain if a visible trail is that of the track-layer or of a wild animal who has crossed the field. Many a handler in a test has erroneously urged his dog onto a visible trail only to realize after the whistle blew that it was not the trail of the track-layer. A well-trained dog in such a situation will "argue" with you, resisting your urging him to follow a wrong trail. An inexperienced dog who has not been properly trained will quickly yield to the desire to please his handler and will overlook the fact that he is being urged to follow a trail other than the one on which he started out. Bearing in mind the fact that you are still training, ignore such visual indications of the location of a trail and concentrate only on reading the dog as he works. If you take this attitude, the presence of such signs can serve to further your understanding of how the dog works, but only after the dog has convinced you otherwise that he is right.

People also will be tempted to look for probable landmarks of the trail to reinforce their confidence. For example, a dog may be working well and seem to be heading directly for a distant tree. His handler guesses that the tree was a landmark used by the track-layer and feels more confident that the dog is right. The handler's guess may be right or wrong, but his feeling of confidence is false. Such guess-work proves to be wrong more often than right. People also frequently have unexplained "hunches" about the length of a leg or the angle of a turn which make them feel the dog has made a mistake. For example, a handler might feel his dog has been working an excessive distance in one direction and missed a turn; or he may feel that a turn the dog made was not as sharp as he expected and that the dog is off the trail. In either case the handler is liable to begin to hold back or subtly guide the dog. If the dog is right and the handler wrong, which is most often the case in situations involving handler guess-work, they are liable to suffer serious set-backs in training. The dog, who *knows* where the trail is, will be confused by his handler holding him back. The handler, who *does not* know where the trail is, will have reduced his confidence in his dog and his training. It is better to let the dog make a mistake and rectify it through training and practice than to cause the dog to make a mistake through erroneous human guess-work.

Self confidence and confidence in the dog are of primary importance in your attitude as you contemplate being certified and entering a tracking test. Many a handler has defeated a capable dog in a test through lack of confidence. We humans are so accustomed to considering ourselves superior to the animal that it is difficult for us to put ourselves in the position of depending, with absolute confidence, upon what we must accept as a superior capability of the dog. If you approach your training program with the attitude that you are learning from the dog as you train him, you will find that you have less trouble developing that essential feeling of confidence.

As in any form of obedience exhibiting, it is important to be thoroughly familiar with the American Kennel Club Regulations as they pertain to tracking tests. These are included in the Obedience Regulations booklet, available upon request from the American Kennel Club, 51 Madison Avenue, New York, N.Y. 10010.

In Chapter 1 of the regulations you will find the rules pertaining to certification of untitled dogs by licensed tracking judges. Most tracking judges have their own way of arranging for and conducting certification tests. Some will test the dog on a fairly simple track under informal conditions. Others conduct certification tests under the same conditions as a regular tracking test.

You should approach certification just as you would a regular test. You should feel that your dog is adequately trained and that you are capable of handling him properly. It will only weaken your confidence if you try for certification before you are ready and then fail.

Although a certification may not be used a second time in the event of failure at your first test, it is permissible to use a signed copy of the original certification if there is more than one test you wish to enter within the six-month time limit of the certification date. Most judges will make copies in such a situation. All such copies must be signed by the judge and bear the same date as the original.

At the end of Chapter 2 of the Obedience Regulations you will find the rules pertaining to performance, and at the end of Chapter 3, the rules pertaining to judging a tracking test. Study these specified regulations and practice with your dog under these conditions so that you will be prepared for the conditions of a test. Do not however limit yourself exclusively to rule-book conditions. Always be prepared for the unexpected at a tracking test. Even at the most carefully planned and conducted tests things often happen to upset ideal situations.

A few years ago an obedience club secured permission to conduct a tracking test on the grounds of a hunt club. The grounds were perfect. The tracks were well arranged and plotted. The first exhibitor was at the first stake and about to start when a fox streaked across the field ahead of her. Next came a pack of baying hounds followed immediately by the thundering herd of mounted hunters. One can only imagine the utter dismay of the handler, judges, spectators and, most of all, the members of the training club who had put so much time and work into planning the test.

This is an extreme example, but anything can, and frequently does happen to disrupt an otherwise perfectly planned test. A wandering farm dog may come around to investigate or challenge the activities of the tracking dog. Flocks of birds may settle on a field in the middle of the tracking area. Wild or domestic animals may cross the tracks, with or without anyone's knowledge. It also happens occasionally that a track-layer becomes confused and inadvertently crosses another track after having walked the one to which he was assigned.

In reading the regulations and practicing according to them, do not let yourself be trapped into a pre-conceived notion of a stereotyped form or pattern of track. Although the regulations state certain specifications for length of a track and the number of legs and turns, with a little imagination one can see there is still a lot of latitude within these specifications.

One of the best possible preparations for entering a tracking test is to attend several of them as a spectator. On the basis of what you observe as a spectator you will have an excellent picture of what to expect when you enter a test as an exhibitor.

The day before a test, an experienced and conscientious judge will look over the areas available and plan the tracks. He will have in mind many pertinent factors. Can each track be plotted so as not to interfere with an adjacent track? Is there a way for each track-layer to leave the area without interfering with another track? Are the turns and location of the article pinpointed by landmarks so that there can be no mistake in judging the exhibitor fairly and accurately? Are the tracks planned in sequence so as to avoid interference and loss of time? Can the tracks be plotted so as to avoid working into a low pocket or toward a wooded area and then away from it? (Ill. 12) Can the tracks be plotted so that there is no chance of any leg paralleling an area downwind which would collect the airborne scent and draw the dog too far off the actual trail? (Ill. 13)

Under the American Kennel Club Regulations the smallest possible area in which a track may be plotted is 150 × 100 yards with an additional 50 yards allowed on each side to avoid interference with another track or geographical obstruction. In such a restricted area Ill. 14 shows how such a track may be plotted. This type of track is more than an economical use of space. In bringing the dog back toward the judges position on the last leg, it also serves to clearly pinpoint the location of the article. This is important because, in the event of failure, it is generally accepted practice to allow the handler to complete the track after his failure has been explained to him and he is told where the article is. It is better, when possible, to open out this type of track with wider angled turns (Ill. 15). A wider track area reduces the chance of interference from downwind scents of other tracks or other legs of the same track.

Once you have been certified and have sent in your entry for

ILL. 12

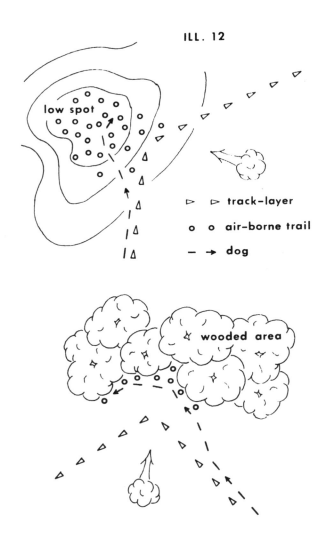

▷   ▷ track-layer

o   o air-borne trail

— → dog

low spot

wooded area

your first test, regular practice becomes most important. Work under as wide a variety of conditions, terrain, weather and time of day as possible. Work as wide a variety of tracks as possible. Practice alone or with someone else, but practice. This will serve to increase your confidence and establish a habit pattern in the mind of your dog which will help you both to overcome any adverse effects resulting from excitement or nervousness when you go into your first test.

The atmosphere at a tracking test is different from that at an obedience trial. You might drive 250 miles to a trial and find yourself among strangers. When you travel a like distance to a tracking test, although you may not know anyone there, you will soon feel you are not among strangers. Perhaps it's the absence of competition, perhaps the mutual recognition of and respect for the months of hard work that have brought you together, but you will enjoy the relaxing company of people with whom you will share the avid hope that *all* the dogs pass the test. You will also enjoy stimulating exchanges with your fellow exhibitors of ideas on training, experiences and problems in training.

When your turn comes someone will call or come for you, depending upon the location and arrangement of the test. This is the time to put the harness on the dog, attaching your regular lead to his collar. Carry the tracking lead in your free hand. If you roll the lead, clasp end out, as you would a ball of twine, or arrange it in a series of loose, flat loops, it may be carried easily without tangling, until you are ready to start your track. A few yards from the first stake the judges will make sure you understand where to start and how to proceed to the second stake. As soon as these preliminaries are over, attach the tracking lead to the harness and remove and pocket the collar and other lead. Proceed to the first stake, drop the tracking lead to the ground behind you and start to work.

At tracking tests one often sees people approach the first stake with the dog still on a regular collar and lead. They put the dog on a sit or stand-stay and put the harness on him. Then, with the dog on a sit or down-stay, they make an elaborate procedure of laying out the whole length of the lead behind the dog. Some will explain that they merely want to make sure the lead cannot get tangled. Others feel that this delaying action gives the dog the

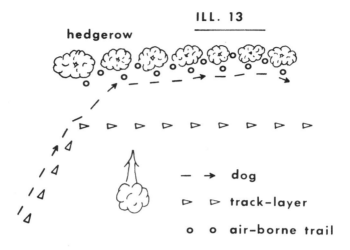

hedgerow

— → dog

▷ ▷ track-layer

o o air-borne trail

Tracking enthusiasts are, by nature, a cordial group of people. Since the atmosphere is not as tense as in the conformation ring or in regular obedience trials, tracking people can be more relaxed in each others' company. Here three fanciers are taking an opportunity to get better acquainted.

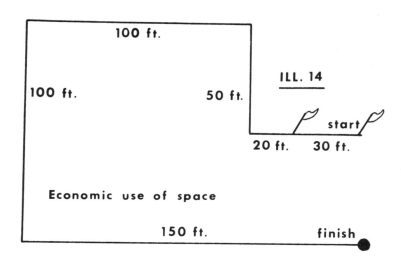

ILL. 14

Economic use of space

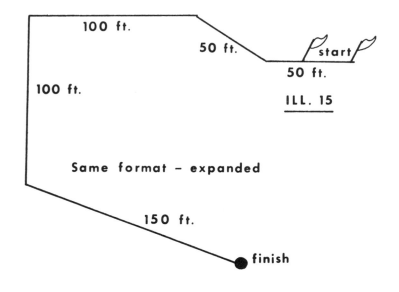

ILL. 15

Same format – expanded

The correct way to start a dog at a tracking test.

Here the dog is beginning to work between the starting stakes.

added advantage of a minute or two during which he may "absorb" the scent of the track-layer at the first stake. Regardless of the reason, this procedure most often reveals a distinct lack of handler confidence.

If the lead has been handled enough in practice without going through a preliminary "laying out", one should have developed an easy, and efficient way of handling it by the time he gets to his first test. As to the idea of the dog absorbing the scent of the track-layer, there is serious reason to question the validity of this. The dog may be aware of the scent of the track-layer at the first stake, but no more so and with no more meaning to him than the presence of any other nearby scent. Far from stimulating interest, dogs more often begin to lose interest at this point. They are liable to get comfortable or bored or curious about something else, or they get fidgety while the handler fusses with the lead. It is better to approach that first stake with the intention of getting right to work before the dog has a chance to be distracted, before the handler allows too many of those last minute doubts to creep into his mind.

Take full advantage of your privilege to make sure the dog is working between the first two stakes. This is the only part of the trail where you will know its exact location. Go through the same procedure you did in early training. With the dog on a shortened lead, point to the ground ahead of him in the direction of the second stake and give him the command to "go find". As he picks up the trail, gradually let the lead slip through your hands under increasing restraint until the dog is pulling you as he should. All the while, drive him to stay with the ground trail until he is past the second stake. From there on you will have to depend upon the dog to follow the track as he has been trained to work. If you make him stay with the ground trail between the first two stakes you will get him into the working attitude you want him to have.

If the minimum length of lead has not been played out by the time the dog reaches the second stake, slow your pace. Allow the dog to continue under uniform restraint until the lead is at least 20 feet long. It is a good idea to have a loop or knot at the 20 foot mark to alert you when it is the right length as the lead slips through your hands. The specific length of lead is not a critical feature in a test and most judges will not make an issue of it unless

The judges and a few of the gallery taking in the action at a tracking test.

"He did it!"—the thrill of passing a tracking test and earning that much-sought-after "T".

the lead is obviously much too long or much too short. It is a good idea in practice to accustom yourself to working within the range of lengths allowed under the regulations.

The tracking regulations state that one may not guide or lead the dog, but may restrain him. This means that so long as the dog is working you must go with him without attempting to influence either his general direction, such as trying to steer him a little to the left or right, or his specific direction, such as attempting to guide him as he casts at a turn. If the dog stops working or, if for some reason, you feel he has made a mistake, you may restrain him until you feel he is working again or has recovered his mistake.

The importance of having learned to read your dog can play a crucial role in your use of the privilege of restraining him in a test. If it is obvious to the judges, who know exactly where the trail is, that you have restrained your dog erroneously or that you will not go with your dog when he is obviously on the trail, they may fail you on your own error. You must be sure that there is good reason for restraint and know when it is right to go with your dog.

Knowledge, understanding and observance of these regulations become critical when you encounter turns. You will have learned to know when your dog has come to or passed a turn. Even if you think you know in which direction the track goes, you must not attempt to guide or lead the dog in any way. As he casts, you may gradually back up, taking care not to pull or lead the dog. Maintain the length of lead as much as possible. Take advantage of his casting behavior and back up a step at a time for a few yards as he works, thus giving him a better chance of picking up the trail again.

If the dog gets tangled in the lead as occasionally happens when casting at a turn, you are allowed to free him. Some dogs will not let the fact that the lead is between their legs bother them and will continue working. In this case, so long as it does not bother the dog, don't stop him from working. Some dogs will free themselves as they continue to work and need no assistance. Others will be disturbed by the lead around or between their legs and may struggle or stop working entirely. In this case, tell the dog to "stay", go to him and free him of the entangled lead. Do this quickly but unexcitedly so that the distraction is kept at a minimum. Then

141

When a dog successfully completes the track, the victory is shared by all. Here the judges and spectators show their pleasure at a contestant passing the test.

urge him to get back to work immediately as you return to your original position.

It would be impossible to anticipate everything that might present a problem at a tracking test. If you have trained and practiced conscientiously, you should be prepared to handle any unexpected circumstance at a tracking test.

The day you pass your first tracking test is one you will never forget. You will experience a real thrill as you see and feel that final burst of energy as your dog zeroes in on the article. You will know in that moment that all the time and effort have been well spent. You will enjoy the heart-felt congratulations of the judges and your fellow exhibitors as you come off the field. Most of all, you will finally know the feeling of real rapport with your dog which comes with the kind of successful team-work it takes to earn that coveted "T".

After the "T"

Practical Tracking—Search and Rescue—Advanced Tracking

By the time you have earned your "T" you will probably have become a real tracking enthusiast. This is the natural result of the time and effort devoted to training your dog, and the satisfaction derived from the insight and rapport you will have gained. Many people, wishing to continue their activities in tracking, continue to practice and enter more tests just for pleasure. Eventually, however, the question arises, "What else can I do in tracking?"

With a little imagination and the companionship of other tracking enthusiasts you can turn practice into interesting and stimulating sessions by creating completely informal tracking problems for the dogs to solve. Here are a few suggestions of what you might do as a track-layer: Simply go for a walk, or "get lost"—wander aimlessly, sit down and rest, weave a little, circle back over your own track, enter a barn or some other building to which the dog may have access and leave by the same door, and drop a few articles along the way. Climb fences or walls that are not insurmountable to the dog. Get in one side and out the other of a car you know won't be there when the dog and handler come after you. Hide in a tree or hayloft or behind a closed door in a building at the end of a track. Once you start, you will find that your imagination provides many such contrived problems.

The men detailed to the care of dogs used on a certain Government project had instructions to work each dog on a track at least three times a week. This got a little boring for the men after a while and they began injecting into the tracks such innovations as described above, and many more. Not only did they enjoy the game of trying to outwit one another, but they were amazed to learn just how much the dogs could do. The increasing difficulty of the tracks also had the effect of sharpening the concentration and spirit of the dogs who seemed to enjoy the "game" as much as the men did.

It is unwise to introduce totally informal tracking such as this until after the dog has earned his "T" or is, to your satisfaction, thoroughly trained. The degree of difficulty should be increased gradually so as not to discourage the dog and jeopardize the spirit of team-work and love of tracking you have acquired. For the same reasons, no physically insurmountable problem should be introduced which will defeat the dog and deprive him of the satisfaction of completing the track.

This sort of informal work is really what is meant by "practical" tracking. It proves the ability of the dog to follow a trial under realistic conditions such as might be encountered in trailing a lost child or criminal.

It happens occasionally that the owner of a tracking dog is called upon for assistance in locating a lost person. There have been times when such dogs were successful. More often, they are not. Most of us would be glad to contribute the services of our tracking dogs in such a situation and this observation concerning chances of success is by no means intended to dissuade anyone from volunteering such a service. It is merely a word of caution about how much to expect in the way of success and gratification.

The failure of a tracking dog in such a situation is not necessarily due to the fact that he was not professionally trained for this sort of work, or that he is incapable. It usually happens that such a dog is brought in as a last resort after all other efforts to locate the lost person have failed. A day or two may have elapsed and the area from which the search started may be so confused and fouled by the tramping about of many people that the dog has little chance of picking up a trail, even with the advantage of a scented article of clothing as a guide.

It also frequently happens that even though the dog is able to pick up and follow the trail, by the time he completes it, the lost person has been found by other means or has returned on his own.

If you are called into such a situation, do not expect too much of even the best trained dog, and do not feel that you have "failed" if the lost person has been found before you finish your part of the job.

This experience is one I have had on more than one occasion. A few years ago a friend of mine became separated from his companions on a hunting trip. When he had been missing for 24 hours I was asked to bring Utah, my German Shepherd, to help search for him. We were taken to the area in which Ted had last been seen and Utah soon picked up the trail and went to work. We had thrashed this way and that through the woods for several miles when we came upon a clearing in which there was a partially finished building. Utah went into and around the building several times. The remains of a recent fire made it obvious that someone had spent the night there. As Utah was working I noticed a farmhouse some distance away and assumed that the trail would eventually go that way, since I believed that Ted would have sought assistance there. When Utah showed no interest in that direction, I went to the house anyway, certain that Ted was either there or had been. No one was at the house and I further assumed that the occupants had taken Ted back to camp or to the local authorities. With this belief we returned to the hunter's camp. There I tied Utah to a nearby tree and settled down to enjoy a cup of coffee and sandwich. Suddenly Utah became very excited, lunging against his tie-line. A few seconds later, who should emerge from the woods but my lost friend, Ted! Utah had never really stopped working and his excitement was prompted by his knowledge that the object of our search was nearby.

In reconstructing Ted's travels and ours, we determined that Utah had been on Ted's trail all the way. The mystery of the two buildings was solved when he told me that he had come upon the unfinished building at night, had gone inside to rest and get warm

145

and dry, and then left at daybreak, unaware of the unlighted house in the half light of dawn, to continue his efforts to find his way back to his companions. He had worked his way back up the mountain to a point whence he was able to get his bearings. Unaware of the search going on for him, he had elected to continue hunting until late afternoon when he returned to camp.

Although Utah "failed" to rescue Ted, he did not actually fail to follow his trail successfully, nor did he fail to recognize the presence of the person whose trail he had been following before any of us knew he was there.

Most people would welcome an opportunity to render a public service. It is only natural to hope for success when such an occasion presents itself, not only for the sake of the lost person, but for self-satisfaction as well. We simply must school ourselves not to regard lack of success necessarily as failure.

A tracking dog may be useful in finding a lost person, but more often the search and rescue approach will be more successful. A search and rescue dog works by winding. He is trained to pick up a human scent and work upwind toward it. In a practical situation such a dog is brought into the area where a lost person is believed to be or was last seen. The handler maneuvers the dog downwind of that area and begins "quartering" with him, walking back and forth across a wide area as the dog winds, gradually working upwind. If the lost person or his trail is there, the dog will eventually pick up the scent and begin working directly toward it, continuing to wind as he goes.

It can readily be seen why this is a more efficient way for a dog to work in searching for a missing person than by tracking alone. A lost child may have wandered aimlessly about the woods for several miles and only be a few hundred yards away. If the child has been injured or is suffering from shock or exposure, the time saved by a dog winding directly to the child, rather than following his trail alone, could be critical.

This is also the way in which military scout dogs are trained to work. Their job is to go out in advance of troop detachments and detect the presence of ambush, snipers or enemy encampments. Obviously, they cannot track in such a situation. They must detect any alien presence by winding.

If you wish to, either for your own amusement or with the

thought of training your dog to search as a potential public service, there is no reason why your tracking dog should not be used to work in this fashion. It is not advisable, however, to try this until after having earned your "T". Once allowed to search by winding, the dog may resort to this in a test and although it will not spoil the dog for tracking as such, your refusal to let him work that way in a test, after you have encouraged him to wind in practice, will amount to a contradiction in training and will confuse or discourage him.

Searching amounts to allowing the dog to seek the scent of a person, whether it is a trail or the person himself, by winding. It is no more possible to teach a dog to search by winding than it is to teach him to track. Winding is as natural to the dog as tracking. By nature, this is the first recourse of the dog when he is seeking something or someone for his own reasons. Search and rescue work may be regarded as an extension of tracking which requires exactly the same fundamentals and principles of training. A dog already trained for tracking will understand what he is supposed to do when he is told to "go find". In the absence of an immediate trail, he will automatically begin to wind in response to the command.

Soundness of training and dependability of the dog are particularly important in search and rescue work since it is usually done off-lead. Since people rarely get lost in open, grassy meadows, search and rescue dogs most often must work in dense, often very rugged, wooded terrain where use of a lead of any sort would hamper both dog and handler. This factor makes it necessary for the handler to pay particular attention to reading the dog visually and controlling him verbally.

If you wish to try the search and rescue technique with your dog, have someone go into a wooded area and stay within a prearranged locale. With the dog on lead, go downwind of this area and begin to walk back and forth, encouraging the dog to "go find". (Ill. 16) The first time or two, give the dog the scent from an article of clothing of the "lost" person. You will note that the dog will immediately begin to seek upwind as you guide him back and forth. When he has picked up the human scent, he will resist your guidance and at this point you must go with him, allowing him to wind freely. Do not remove the lead until you are sure the dog will respond reliably to verbal control.

147

At first, have your lost person enter the area so that there will be no trail between his hiding place and the dog. Later, have him enter the woods so that the dog is bound to pick up the scent from the trail before the scent directly from the individual. (Ill. 17) This might best be done on a day when the wind velocity is light. You will note that the dog picks up the trail scent by winding and once he has worked his way to it, he will follow the trail by tracking. If, while working the trail, he picks up the human scent upwind, he will abandon the trail and proceed directly to the person, resorting once again to winding.

Such experiments are not training in the truest sense of the word, and, obviously, such work may not be done successfully with a dog who has not already been thoroughly trained to understand what is expected of him when he is given the command to "go find".

There is no reason why you should not experiment with this approach to trailing. Remember, however, that even though your dog may perform well, there are aspects of this highly specialized type of work which require experience and handler training as well as dog training. Successful training for this type of work can only be acquired under the direct guidance of an experienced instructor and requires many hours of rugged field work. Professional search and rescue handlers must be trained in visual trailing and scouting techniques. They must have a thorough knowledge of first aid and emergency survival; and they, as well as their dogs must be in top physical condition. Obviously, serious search and rescue training is not for the average dog or the average handler.

Advanced Tracking (TDX)

The ever increasing popularity of tracking in the 1960's created in the minds of many people the desire for an Advanced Tracking test which would carry with it an officially recognized obedience title of TDX. Consideration of this was on the agenda of the American Kennel Club Advisory Committee which met during 1968 to work out revisions of the Obedience Regulations. Unfortunately, limitations of time and the press of other matters made it impossible for them to give full consideration to advanced tracking at that time.

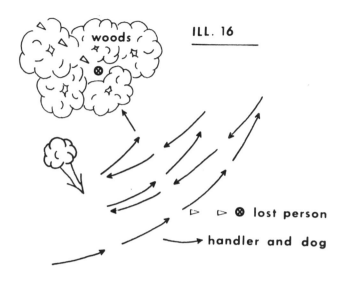

ILL. 16

▷ ▷ ⊗ lost person

handler and dog

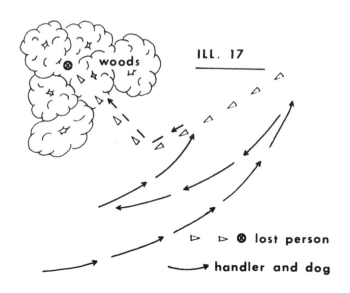

ILL. 17

▷ ▷ ⊗ lost person

handler and dog

TYPICAL ADVANCED TRACK

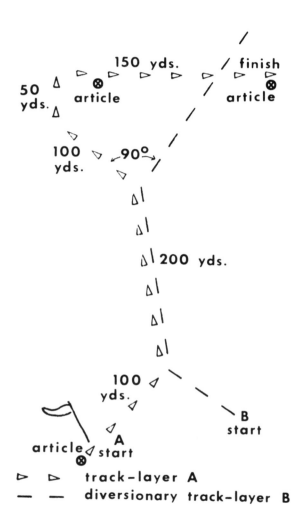

track–layer A

diversionary track-layer B

The subject of Advanced Tracking was assigned to a Committee who consulted me for suggestions about how such a test might be conducted within a reasonable limitation of space, with a certain degree of uniformity for each exhibitor, and with requirements of a more practical and realistic nature to test the capabilities of a well-trained tracking dog. The final diagram of the proposed Advanced Tracking test appears in this book.

We considered various capabilities of the trained tracking dog which are not demonstrated in a regular test.

a) His ability to determine, without guidance, the initial direction of the trail once he has been given the scent of the track-layer.

b) His ability to distinguish between individuals and stay on a designated trail despite the intrusion and interference of another person.

c) His ability to follow a trail over a variety of ground conditions.

To test the dog's ability to pick up the beginning of a trail without guidance, we eliminated the second of the starting stakes. The beginning of the track is indicated by one stake and an article of clothing such as a shoe, hat, sweater or scarf dropped on the ground by the track-layer as he starts the track. The article is pointed out by the judge to the handler who takes the dog to it, allowing him to get the scent from it, and then tells him to "go find". The task of the dog is to find and proceed to work the trail. The handler is given no clue as to the direction of the track from the first stake and the dog must determine it alone.

In considering how to test the dog's ability to distinguish between individuals, we reverted to a way dogs had been tested in experiments conducted in a Government Research project to establish the fact that the dog possesses this capability. One of the problems with which we confronted the dog was to have two track-layers walk the same track and branch off at right angles. In order to be sure we knew which track-layer the dog was following, the dog was started on the trail of one track-layer and the diversion was introduced at least 100 yards down-trail. The dog proceeded on the double track to the point of separation of the two track-layers where he had to make the choice of which trail to follow. This simple test contributed a large portion of the proof that the dog can make the distinction between individuals. A well trained dog

151

will rarely be confused by a second track-layer and will rarely make the error of following the diversionary trail at the point of separation. This same test was incorporated into the proposed Advanced Tracking test along with the additional challenge of having the diversionary track-layer cross the initial trail at a later point.

As much variety of terrain as possible is included in each track pasture, plowed fields, over-grown or uncultivated land. As many specific challenges as possible are included—shallow streams or ditches, hard-surfaced or dirt roads, bridges, etc.

On the last leg of the track two articles are dropped rather than one, to test the dog's willingness to continue working even though he has found an article.

Subsequently several Advanced Tracking tests sanctioned by the American Kennel Club were conducted under these specifications. These were the first step in getting an Advanced Tracking or TDX title now officially offered by AKC.

In the first offerings of this test, it was surprising how few dogs passed. Those who did pass gave beautiful demonstrations of how a well-trained tracking team can and should work. There was more to be learned, however, from the failures. Most of the dogs entered in these tests were trained well enough to have passed. Most of the dogs who failed were defeated by the confusion of the handlers rather than the difficulty of the test itself. The two major stumbling blocks were the start and the entrance or departure of the diversionary track-layer.

In the failures at the start, some of the handlers, unaccustomed to having no second stake to guide them as their dogs sought out the trail, either became confused and followed the dog in the first direction he turned, without taking proper note of whether he was tracking or casting. Others, for one reason or another, had some fixed idea in their own minds about what direction the track probably went and refused to let the dog work it out for himself. Some tried to guide the dog in the wrong direction. Others held the dog back when he was straining to go the right way. When asked afterwards why they had conducted themselves as they did, most of them admitted that they thought they knew which way the trail went. This, of course, is one of the greatest pitfalls in handling—trying to out-guess the track-layer instead of trusting in the capability and training of the dog.

Of the dogs who failed in these early tests because of the diversionary track, about an equal number failed at the introduction of the diversion as did at the departure. Most of the handlers, knowing there was a diversionary track, were aware of the fact that their dogs were at one of these two points due to what appeared to be an unnatural confusion on the part of the dog. Confused themselves, not knowing from which direction the diversion came or in what direction he departed, they failed to read the subtle differences in the way the dog worked when checking each trail. In many such instances the spectators could see the difference even at a distance. Many of the handlers also neglected to take advantage of their option to give the dog the scent again from the starting article which they may carry with them for this purpose—to remind the dog when he appears to be confused as may occur with the interference of a diversionary track-layer.

These early Advanced Tracking tests proved to be tests of good handling as well as tests of good tracking dogs. It is probable that more of the dogs entered would have passed if their handlers had read them properly and had more confidence in them and their training. The validity of this assumption was proved by several of them who came back a year or two later and, having profited from their first experience, passed their second test with flying colors.

The Board of Directors of AKC ultimately approved a Tracking Dog Excellent test which became effective on March 1, 1980. The official rules for this test appear at the end of this chapter.

Except for practicing under the conditions specified by the requirements of the Advanced Tracking test itself, there is no way to train a dog specifically for this test which is not included in training him for a regular tracking test. The only real difference between the two tests is in the necessity for a higher quality of training and greater degree of confidence on the part of the handler. The Advanced Tracking test does not include anything that the dog cannot do without additional training. It merely offers additional challenges to his willingness to work and his understanding of what is expected of him as determined by his training. There are many well-trained dogs with confident handlers who have only been trained for and entered in regular tracking tests who could pass the Advanced Test with no additional training. Whether or not you are preparing for an Advanced Tracking test, this is a good exercise to use in practice with a trained tracking dog.

When preparing to enter an Advanced Tracking test you should go back to working staked or known tracks so that you know exactly when to correct and when to praise. Practicing the start of an advanced track, with no second stake to guide you, should be approached in much the same way as you introduced the dog to turns. Leave an article of clothing at the first stake and walk the track. When you approach the first stake with the dog, make sure you walk toward it so that you are not facing the direction of the trail. Indicate the article to the dog, let him get the scent from it and encourage his interest in it. Then give him the command to "go find." Do not give him any further guidance. Let him cast in any direction and repeat the command as he casts. If he has not picked up the trail by the time you know he has crossed it several times, bring him back to the starting point, give him the scent from the article again and start him in search of the trail once more with repeated commands. Encourage him when he shows his first indication of having picked up the trail, but go with him only when he has committed himself by actively pulling you along in the right direction.

In practicing with the dog on the challenge of a diversionary track you will require the assistance of another person to act either as the track-layer or diversion. Here again, it is important to practice on staked or known tracks so that you can praise and correct effectively. Without any guidance, the dog must be allowed to make the decision, to the extent of clear-cut committment, at each point of introduction and departure of the diversionary track-layer. He should be encouraged verbally while making any such decision but must not be guided by lead, correction or praise until he has committed himself. If he makes the correct decision praise him and drive him on with commands and encouragement. If he makes the wrong decision guide him back to the junction of the two tracks, give him the scent from the starting article, move back and let him work it out again. A dog with good early training will soon understand what is required of him and may eventually handle this challenge so well that it is difficult for you to determine, from his working behavior, the location of a diversion anywhere along a given track.

If you introduce these new challenges gradually as part of routine "fun" tracking practice, the dog will soon come to accept them and meet them as a normal aspect of tracking. If you treat these new elements as separate training projects, you may tend to over-do it and jeopardize the continuity of smooth team-work you have developed through earlier training and practice, to say nothing of the risk of taking some of the pleasure out of your practice sessions.

As you prepare for advanced tests you may also introduce multiple articles, changes of terrain and specific obstacles such as hard-surfaced roads to be crossed, if you have not already done so in previous fun practice.

Whether you are preparing for advanced tests or not, always maintain a spirit of team-work and mutual enjoyment with your dog. This is the true sport of tracking—the joy and satisfaction of working together as a team.

American Kennel Club Tracking Regulations

Section 1. **Tracking Test.** This test shall be for dogs not less than six months of age, and must be judged by two judges. With each entry form for a licensed or member tracking test for a dog that has not passed an AKC tracking test there must be filed an original written statement, dated within six months of the date the test is to be held, signed by a person who has been approved by The American Kennel Club to judge tracking tests, certifying that the dog is considered by him to be ready for such a test. These original statements cannot be used again and must be submitted to The American Kennel Club with the entry forms. Written permission to waive or modify this requirement may be granted by The American Kennel Club in unusual circumstances. Tracking tests are open to all dogs that are otherwise eligible under these Regulations.

This test cannot be given at a dog show or obedience trial. The duration of this test may be one day or more within a 15 day period after the original date in the event of an unusually large entry or other unforeseen emergency, provided that the change of date is satisfactory to the exhibitors affected.

Section 2. **T.D. Title.** The American Kennel Club will issue a Tracking Dog certificate to a registered dog, and will permit the use of the letters "T.D." after the name of each dog which has been certified by the two judges to have passed a licensed or member tracking test in which at least three dogs actually participated.

The owner of a dog holding both the U.D. and T.D. titles may use the letters "U.D.T." after the name of the dog, signifying "Utility Dog Tracker."

Section 3. **Tracking.** The tracking test must be performed with the dog on leash, the length of the track to be not less than 440 yards nor more than 500 yards, the scent to be not less than one half hour nor more than two hours old and that of a stranger who will leave an inconspicuous glove or wallet, dark in color, at the end of the track where it must be found by the dog and picked up by the dog or handler. The article must be approved in advance by the judges. The tracklayer will follow the track which has been staked out with flags a day or more earlier, collecting all the flags on the way with the exception of one flag at the start of the track and one flag about 30 yards from the start of the track to indicate the direction of the track; then deposit the article at the end of the track and leave the course, proceeding straight ahead at least 50 feet. The tracklayer must wear his own shoes which, if not having leather soles, must have uppers of fabric or leather. The dog shall wear a harness to which is attached a leash between 20 and 40 feet in length. The handler shall follow the dog at a distance of not less than 20 feet, and the dog shall not be guided by the handler. The dog may be restrained by the handler, but any leading or guiding of the dog constitutes grounds for calling the handler off and marking the dog "Failed." A dog may, at the handler's option, be given one, and only one, second chance to take the scent between the two flags, provided it has not passed the second flag.

Section 4. **Tracking Tests.** A person who is qualified to judge Obedience Trials is not necessarily capable of judging a tracking test. Tracking judges must be familiar with the various conditions that may exist when a dog is required to work a scent trail. Scent conditions, weather, lay of the land, ground cover, and wind, must be taken into consideration, and a thorough knowledge of this work is necessary.

One or both of the judges must personally lay out each track, a day or so before the test, so as to be completely familiar with the location of the track, landmarks and ground conditions. At least two of the right angle turns shall be well out in the open where there are no fences or other boundaries to guide the dog. No part of any track shall follow along any fence or boundary within 15 yards of such boundary. The track shall include at least two right angle turns and should include more than two such turns so that the dog may be observed working in different wind directions. Acute angle turns should be avoided whenever possible. No conflicting tracks shall be laid. No track shall cross any body of water. No part of any track shall be laid within 75 yards of any other track. In the case of two tracks going in opposite directions, however, the first flags of these tracks may be as close as 50 yards from each other. The judges shall make sure that the track is no less than 440 yards nor more than 500 yards and that the tracklayer is a stranger to the dog in each case. It is the judges' responsibility to instruct the tracklayer to insure that each track is properly laid and that each tracklayer carries a copy of the chart with him in laying the track. The judges must approve the article to be left at the end of each track, must make sure that it is thoroughly impregnated with the tracklayer's scent, and must see that the tracklayer's shoes meet the requirements of these regulations.

There is no time limit provided the dog is working, but a dog that is off the track and is clearly not working should not be given any minimum time, but should be marked Failed. The handler may not be given any assistance by the judges or anyone else. If a dog is not tracking it shall not be marked Passed even though it may have found the article. In case of unforseen circumstances, the judges may in rare cases, at their own discretion, give a handler and his dog a second chance on a new track. A track for each dog entered shall be plotted on the ground by one or both judges not less than one day before the test, the track being marked by flags which the tracklayer can follow readily on the day of the test. A chart of each track shall be made up in duplicate, showing the approximate length in yards of each leg, and major landmarks and boundaries, if any. Both of these charts shall be marked at the time the dog is tracking, one by each of the judges, so as to show the approximate course followed by the dog. The judges shall sign their charts and show on each whether the dog "Passed" or "Failed," the time the tracklayer started, the time the dog started and finished tracking, a brief description of ground, wind and weather conditions, the wind direction, and a note of any steep hills or valleys.

The Club or Tracking Test Secretary, after a licensed or member tracking test, shall forward the two copies of the judges' marked charts, the entry forms with certifications attached, and a marked and certified copy of the catalog pages or sheets listing the dogs entered in the tracking test, to The American Kennel Club so as to reach its office within seven days after the close of the test.

Section 1. **Tracking Dog Excellent Test.** This test shall be for dogs that have earned the title T.D., and must be judged by two judges. The maximum number of dogs two judges may be asked to test in one day is five. Dogs that have earned this title T.D.X. may continue to compete. This test cannot be given at a dog show or obedience trial. In the event of an unforeseen emergency, the duration of this test may be more than one day but within a 15 day period after the original date, provided that the extension of the test is satisfactory to the exhibitors affected.

Section 2. **T.D.X.** The American Kennel Club will issue a Tracking Dog Excellent certificate to a registered dog, and will permit the use of the letters "T.D.X." after the name of each dog that has been certified by the two judges to have passed a licensed or member club Tracking Dog Excellent Test in which at least two dogs actually participated.

The owner of the dog holding the "U.D." and "T.D.X." titles may use the letters "U.D.T.X." after the name of the dog, signifying "Utility Dog Tracker Excellent."

Section 3. **The T.D.X. Track.** The Tracking Dog Excellent Test must be performed with dog on leash. The length of the track shall not be less than 800 yards nor more than 1000 yards. The scent shall be not less than three hours nor more than four hours old and must be that of a stranger. The actual track, laid earlier, shall be crossed at two widely separated places by more recent tracks.

Four personal dissimilar articles, well impregnated with the tracklayer's scent, will be dropped by the tracklayer at designated points directly on the track. The articles must be approved in advance by the judges.

At a point more than 75 yards from the start of the track the tracklayer will be given a map of the track. He will place one article at the starting flag then follow the track which has been staked out with flags a day or more earlier. Along the way of the actual track he will collect all but the first flag. He will drop the remaining three articles directly on the track at points designated on the map. The articles shall not be dropped within 30 yards of a turn or cross track. After dropping the last article the tracklayer will proceed straight ahead for at least 30 yards and then leave the field.

One hour to one hour and a half after the actual tracklaying has been completed the judges will instruct two people, strangers to the dog, to start from a given point, walking side by side about four feet apart, and follow each of the two cross tracks which have been staked out with flags a day or more earlier, collecting all of the flags along the way.

While tracking the dog shall wear a harness to which is attached a leash 20 feet to 40 feet in length. To avoid entanglement the leash may be dropped during the tracking but must be retrieved. The dog must be under the handler's control at all times. At the start of the track the dog will be given ample time to take the scent and begin tracking. No guidance of any kind is to be employed by the handler while starting the dog on the track. Since there is no second flag in this test, the handler must wait for the dog to commit itself before he leaves the starting flag. Once the handler has left the starting flag the test has begun and shall not be restarted. The handler may pick up the article at the starting flag and may use it, as well as subsequent articles, to give the scent to the dog while on the track. Where obstacles, barriers, or terrain demand, a handler may aid the dog, but any leading or guiding of the dog shall constitute grounds for calling the handler off and marking the dog "Failed."

Should the dog follow one of the cross tracks for a distance of more than 50 yards, the dog is to be marked "Failed." The dog must follow the track and either indicate or retrieve the second, third and fourth articles. In order for the dog to be marked "Passed," these articles must be presented to the judge, when the track is completed.

Section 4. **Essentials for a T.D.X. Test.** AKC tracking judges may be approved to judge this test. Such judges must have experience with advanced tracking and be familiar with conditions that present themselves when a dog is required to work a scent trail. Scent conditions such as weather, age, terrain, ground cover changes, natural as well as man-made obstacles, cross tracks, streams and roads must be taken into consideration when judging advanced tracking.

Both judges must personally lay out each track a day or so before the test in order to be completely familiar with the location of the track, landmarks and ground conditions.

The track shall be not less than 800 yards nor more than 1000 yards and shall contain at least three turns and two widely separated double cross tracks. The cross tracks shall intersect the actual track at right angles. All types of terrain and cover, including gulleys, plowed land, woods and vegetation of any density may be used. Natural obstacles such as streams or man-made obstacles such as hedgerows, fences, bridges, or lightly traveled roads may also be used. No portion of any track, including the tracklayer's escape route or the escape route of the cross tracklayers, may be within 75 yards of any other track.

It is the judges' responsibility to instruct the tracklayer and the cross tracklayers so as to insure that each track is properly laid and that they each carry a copy of the chart with them while laying track.

Conclusion

THE main purpose of this book has been to put together all the accumulated knowledge and experience I have gained over nearly two decades of concentrated professional work with tracking dogs, and to pass it on for the benefit of those who wish to better understand, train and work with their dogs.

Tracking is not a mysterious complicated subject. For the dog it is an instinct as fundamental as eating and sleeping. This simple, bald fact is the one that often is overlooked by those who train dogs in tracking. Being unmindful of this fact often leads people into complex theories and speculations which can never be proved. These theories and speculations in turn lead to strange and complicated ways of training, to say nothing of creating all sorts of concerns about what the dog can't or won't do and why.

Accept the fact of the dog's instinct and approach training from the standpoint of teaching him to work on command, and you have the foundation of good training. Follow through with that attitude and you should attain your goal.

Tracking is one of the most challenging and satisfying forms of dog training. A unique depth of understanding and respect develops between a good tracking dog and his handler. This rapport cannot be explained. It simply happens. You will feel it the first time you go out on a blind track and suddenly you *know* your dog is going to complete that track.

My years of work in this field have been both enlightening and rewarding, and have given me the unshakeable convictions set forth in this book.

I have often experienced personal satisfaction in proving the validity of these convictions. But most gratifying of all is seeing someone else accept them, work and train on the basis of them, and enjoy the rewards of success and companionship that can come of working with a well-trained tracking dog.

It is to the purpose of encouraging and guiding those interested in attaining this sort of satisfaction and pleasure from tracking that this book is finally dedicated.

BIBLIOGRAPHY

ALL OWNERS of pure-bred dogs will benefit themselves and their dogs by enriching their knowledge of breeds and of canine care, training, breeding, psychology and other important aspects of dog management. The following list of books covers further reading recommended by judges, veterinarians, breeders, trainers and other authorities. Books may be obtained at the finer book stores and pet shops, or through Howell Book House Inc., publishers, New York.

BREED BOOKS

AFGHAN HOUND, Complete	Miller & Gilbert
AIREDALE, New Complete	Edwards
AKITA, Complete	Linderman & Funk
ALASKAN MALAMUTE, Complete	Riddle & Seeley
BASSET HOUND, New Complete	Braun
BLOODHOUND, Complete	Brey & Reed
BOXER, Complete	Denlinger
BRITTANY SPANIEL, Complete	Riddle
BULLDOG, New Complete	Hanes
BULL TERRIER, New Complete	Eberhard
CAIRN TERRIER, New Complete	Marvin
CHESAPEAKE BAY RETRIEVER, Complete	Cherry
CHIHUAHUA, Complete	Noted Authorities
COCKER SPANIEL, New	Kraeuchi
COLLIE, New	Official Publication of the Collie Club of America
DACHSHUND, The New	Meistrell
DALMATIAN, The	Treen
DOBERMAN PINSCHER, New	Walker
ENGLISH SETTER, New Complete	Tuck, Howell & Graef
ENGLISH SPRINGER SPANIEL, New	Goodall & Gasow
FOX TERRIER, New	Nedell
GERMAN SHEPHERD DOG, New Complete	Bennett
GERMAN SHORTHAIRED POINTER, New	Maxwell
GOLDEN RETRIEVER, New Complete	Fischer
GORDON SETTER, Complete	Look
GREAT DANE, New Complete	Noted Authorities
GREAT DANE, The—Dogdom's Apollo	Draper
GREAT PYRENEES, Complete	Strang & Giffin
IRISH SETTER, New Complete	Eldredge & Vanacore
IRISH WOLFHOUND, Complete	Starbuck
JACK RUSSELL TERRIER, Complete	Plummer
KEESHOND, New Complete	Cash
LABRADOR RETRIEVER, New Complete	Warwick
LHASA APSO, Complete	Herbel
MALTESE, Complete	Cutillo
MASTIFF, History and Management of the	Baxter & Hoffman
MINIATURE SCHNAUZER, New	Kiedrowski
NEWFOUNDLAND, New Complete	Chern
NORWEGIAN ELKHOUND, New Complete	Wallo
OLD ENGLISH SHEEPDOG, Complete	Mandeville
PEKINGESE, Quigley Book of	Quigley
PEMBROKE WELSH CORGI, Complete	Sargent & Harper
POODLE, New	Irick
POODLE CLIPPING AND GROOMING BOOK, Complete	Kalstone
PORTUGUESE WATER DOG, Complete	Braund & Miller
ROTTWEILER, Complete	Freeman
SAMOYED, New Complete	Ward
SCOTTISH TERRIER, New Complete	Marvin
SHETLAND SHEEPDOG, The New	Riddle
SHIH TZU, Joy of Owning	Seranne
SHIH TZU, The (English)	Dadds
SIBERIAN HUSKY, Complete	Demidoff
TERRIERS, The Book of All	Marvin
WEIMARANER, Guide to the	Burgoin
WEST HIGHLAND WHITE TERRIER, Complete	Marvin
WHIPPET, Complete	Pegram
YORKSHIRE TERRIER, Complete	Gordon & Bennett

BREEDING

ART OF BREEDING BETTER DOGS, New	Onstott
BREEDING YOUR OWN SHOW DOG	Seranne
HOW TO BREED DOGS	Whitney
HOW PUPPIES ARE BORN	Prine
INHERITANCE OF COAT COLOR IN DOGS	Little

CARE AND TRAINING

BEYOND BASIC DOG TRAINING	Bauman
COUNSELING DOG OWNERS, Evans Guide for	Evans
DOG OBEDIENCE, Complete Book of	Saunders
NOVICE, OPEN AND UTILITY COURSES	Saunders
DOG CARE AND TRAINING FOR BOYS AND GIRLS	Saunders
DOG NUTRITION, Collins Guide to	Collins
DOG TRAINING FOR KIDS	Benjamin
DOG TRAINING, Koehler Method of	Koehler
DOG TRAINING Made Easy	Tucker
GO FIND! Training Your Dog to Track	Davis
GROOMING DOGS FOR PROFIT	Gold
GUARD DOG TRAINING, Koehler Method of	Koehler
MOTHER KNOWS BEST—The Natural Way to Train Your Dog	Benjamin
OPEN OBEDIENCE FOR RING, HOME AND FIELD, Koehler Method of	Koehler
STONE GUIDE TO DOG GROOMING FOR ALL BREEDS	Stone
SUCCESSFUL DOG TRAINING, The Pearsall Guide to	Pearsall
TEACHING DOG OBEDIENCE CLASSES—Manual for Instructors	Volhard & Fisher
TOY DOGS, Kalstone Guide to Grooming All	Kalstone
TRAINING THE RETRIEVER	Kersley
TRAINING TRACKING DOGS, Koehler Method of	Koehler
TRAINING YOUR DOG—Step by Step Manual	Volhard & Fisher
TRAINING YOUR DOG TO WIN OBEDIENCE TITLES	Morsell
TRAIN YOUR OWN GUN DOG, How to	Goodall
UTILITY DOG TRAINING, Koehler Method of	Koehler
VETERINARY HANDBOOK, Dog Owner's Home	Carlson & Giffin

GENERAL

A DOG'S LIFE	Burton & Allaby
AMERICAN KENNEL CLUB 1884-1984—A Source Book	American Kennel Club
CANINE TERMINOLOGY	Spira
COMPLETE DOG BOOK, The	Official Publication of American Kennel Club
DOG IN ACTION, The	Lyon
DOG BEHAVIOR, New Knowledge of	Pfaffenberger
DOG JUDGE'S HANDBOOK	Tietjen
DOG PSYCHOLOGY	Whitney
DOGSTEPS, The New	Elliott
DOG TRICKS	Haggerty & Benjamin
EYES THAT LEAD—Story of Guide Dogs for the Blind	Tucker
FRIEND TO FRIEND—Dogs That Help Mankind	Schwartz
FROM RICHES TO BITCHES	Shattuck
HAPPY DOG/HAPPY OWNER	Siegal
IN STITCHES OVER BITCHES	Shattuck
JUNIOR SHOWMANSHIP HANDBOOK	Brown & Mason
OUR PUPPY'S BABY BOOK (blue or pink)	
SUCCESSFUL DOG SHOWING, Forsyth Guide to	Forsyth
WHY DOES YOUR DOG DO THAT?	Bergman
WILD DOGS in Life and Legend	Riddle
WORLD OF SLED DOGS, From Siberia to Sport Racing	Coppinger